THE ATLANTIC CRITICAL STUDIES

ERNEST HEMINGWAY'S

A Farewell to Arms

THE ATLANTIC CRITICAL STUDIES

ERNEST HEMINGWAY'S

A Farewell to Arms

P.G. Rama Rao

ATLANTIC

PUBLISHERS & DISTRIBUTORS (P) LTD

Published by

ATLANTIC

PUBLISHERS & DISTRIBUTORS (P) LTD

7/22, Ansari Road, Darya Ganj, New Delhi-110002
Phones : +91-11-40775252, 40775214, 23273880, 23275880
Fax : +91-11-23285873
Web : www.atlanticbooks.com
E-mail : orders@atlanticbooks.com

Branch Office: Chennai
Phones : +91-44-48531784, 28291383
E-mail : chennai@atlanticbooks.com

Printed & bound in India by Atlantic Print Services

General Preface

The Atlantic Critical Studies are study-aids modelled on the study-aids available in England and America, among other places, and are primarily meant for the students of English Literature of Indian universities.

However, in consideration of the local conditions and the various constraints under which our students have to study—non-availability of relevant critical books, dearth of foreign and Indian journals, inaccessibility to good, well-equipped libraries, just to mention a few of them—the models have been considerably improved upon, both qualitatively and quantitatively.

Thus, while these studies are meant to be comprehensive and self-sufficient, the distinguished scholars who have prepared these study materials, have taken special care to combine lucidity and profundity in their treatment of the texts.

The Select Bibliography at the end is meant not only to acknowledge the sources used but also to help a student in the pursuit of further studies if s/he wants to.

Atlantic Publishers & Distributors (P) Ltd., believe in quality and excellence. These studies will only reconfirm it.

MOHIT K. RAY
Chief Editor [English Literature]
Atlantic Publishers & Distributors (P) Ltd.,
New Delhi

Preface

I am beholden to Dr. K.R. Gupta and Dr. Mohit K. Ray for asking me to write critical study of Hemingway's *A Farewell to Arms*.

In the late 1960s, I wrote my Ph.D. Thesis on "The Narrative Technique of Ernest Hemingway" at the American Studies Research Centre, Hyderabad, where I was a Research Fellow in 1968 and 1969. One of my earlier books is based on my research, which was published by S. Chand & Company Ltd., New Delhi, and released at the All India English Teachers' Conference, Madras, in the last week of December 1979. I studied the Hemingway manuscripts in the John F. Kennedy Presidential Library, Boston, the New York Public Library, the Newberry Library, Chicago, the H.R.C. Library, Austin (Texas), the Bancroft Library, Berkeley (Cal), and the Library of Congress, Washington DC, in 1981-82. Since most of the Hemingway papers are in the Kennedy Library, I spent most of that year in Boston, where I was a Fulbright Adjunct Professor in the Department of English, University of Massachusetts, Boston.

I had the privilege of meeting Charles Scribner Jr., Malcolm Cowley, Alfred Rice and other Associates of Hemingway, participating in the Hemingway Conference in Harvard Club, New York, and meeting with leading Hemingway scholars there, and in the MLA conference. Later, I attended the

Second International Hemingway Conference at Lignano Sabbiadoro (Italy), and acted as Rapporteur in June 1986. In June 1988, I participated in the Third International Hemingway Conference at Schruns (Austria), and presented papers in two sessions.

I lectured on Hemingway in the English Department, Edinburgh University, in October 1986, during my visit to the Oxford and Edinburgh Universities as a British Council visitor. In 1993 I visited the U.S.A. on a Fulbright American Research Fellowship and studied the manuscripts of the posthumously published novel, *The Garden of Eden.* I was again an Adjunct Professor in the American Studies Department of the University of Massachusetts, Boston, where I lectured on the Revisions in the manuscripts of *The Garden of Eden.* In October 1993 I made a lecture tour of several universities in the U.S.A., and Canada [University of Vermont, University of Puget Sound, Tacoma (WA.), the New School of Social Sciences, New York, Reed College, Portland (Oregon), and the University of British Columbia, Vancouver (Canada)].

After my retirement from Utkal University, Bhubaneswar (Orissa), in February 1995, I acted as a Visiting Fellow at the American Studies Research Centre, Hyderabad, where I organized a National Seminar on 'Hemingway and Film' in November 1995.

Having involved myself with Hemingway studies for nearly four decades, writing and lecturing on him, I was delighted when I was asked to write the critical study on *A Farewell to Arms*.

A Farewell to Arms is not only one of Hemingway's best novels but also one of the best novels on love in the time of war. I have tried to study this novel against the background of his total work published during his lifetime. This gives us a proper perspective, and unfolds its themes, characters, techniques and meanings in the appropriate light.

The important thing for us to consider is not why Hemingway wrote what he wrote, but how he wrote it, for a writer writes from his experience and the reader shares that experience. It would be unfair to find fault with a writer for writing about certain things and not writing about certain other things for he has the freedom to choose his subjects like any of us.

If I have succeeded in rousing the interest of the reader well enough to make him read this novel in depth and enjoy the experience, I have not written in vain.

P.G. Rama Rao

Contents

1

Ernest Hemingway: His Life and Works

Ernest Miller Hemingway was born on July 21, 1899 in Oak Park, Illinois. His father was Clarence Edmonds Hemingway, a general medical practitioner, who was the eldest son of Anson T. Hemingway, a civil war veteran with prosperous real estate business in Chicago. Dr. Hemingway was a powerfully built man with a barrel chest, and stood six feet tall. He was passionately interested in fishing and hunting. These were qualities which his son Ernest Hemingway was to inherit later.

Ernest Hemingway's mother was Grace Hall, who had a good contralto voice and taught music. Her father, Ernest Hall, was also a civil war veteran like Anson. Ernest had an elder sister, Marcelline, who was a year and a half older, and three younger sisters, Ursula, Madeleine, and Carol, and a kid brother, Leicester, the youngest of the lot.

Ernest was a good looking boy with dimples in both his cheeks and a talent for making up stories and an occasional verse. He inherited his mother's love of music and sang regularly in the church.

He attended the Oak Park High School from 1913 to 1917. After completing High School where he wrote for the school magazine, he moved to Kansas city. He was a cub reporter for *Kansas City Star* in 1917. His desire to join the army remained unfulfilled owing to his eye problem. He was disqualified in the tests because of his weak left eye and had to be content with a position in the Italian Red Cross Ambulance Corps. The Austro-Italian war was going on at that time and his assignment was at Fossalta, a badly battered village on the river, Piave. Here, on July 8, 1918, he was severely wounded in both the legs by a trench mortar while carrying a supply of cigarettes, chocolate, and postcards for the soldiers. Close to him was a soldier more severely wounded and crying in great agony for help. Ernest carried him towards the command post and lost consciousness on the way. Three years later, a grateful nation honoured him with the high military decorations—*Medaglia d'Argento al Valore Militare* and *Croce ad Merito di Guerra.*

He recuperated in the Red Cross Hospital in Milan, where he fell in love with one of the nurses called Agnes Von Kurowsky. He returned to Oak Park as a wounded hero in 1919. Rejected by Agnes, he found comfort in writing.

The delegates to the second International Hemingway Conference in June 1986 at Lignano on the Adriatic, of whom I was one, were profoundly moved by the way Italy still honoured the memory of Hemingway. There is a memorial for him at *Fossalta di Piave*, where he was wounded in 1918. We were given civic receptions in five cities; the Italian aristocracy played host to us in four villas; and the Italian army held a memorable reception for us with army band and military ceremony. All this was in homage to the memory of Hemingway.

His wound at *Fossalta di Piave* left an indelible scar on his psyche, which resulted in what is called "Repetitive Compulsion". For a long time he could not sleep in the nights and had to keep a light in his room. He tried hard to overcome his fear of death by seeking it again and again and staring it in the face. He dared danger and death all his life. This accounts for the presence of war, violence, death, darkness and *nada* (Spanish for 'nothingness') in his fiction.

In 1920 he moved to Toronto and wrote for the *Toronto Star Weekly*. Later he travelled to Chicago where he met two famous writers of that time—Sherwood Anderson, the fiction writer, and Carl Sandberg, the poet. Anderson had just returned from Paris and was full of stories of well-known British and European writers. Hemingway was thrilled.

In September 1921 he married Hadley Richardson and, in December, sailed with her for Paris as the European correspondent for the *Toronto Star Weekly*. He was armed with letters of introduction from Sherwood Anderson and met well-known literary figures like Gertrude Stein, Ezra Pound, John Dos Passos, James Joyce, Ford Madox Ford, and Scott Fitzgerald there. Gertrude Stein's salon was the meeting place for literary personalities, and Hemingway soon became a regular visitor there. He was a regular visitor to Sylvia Beach's bookstore, Shakespeare and Company, where he read English and European classics avidly.

As the European correspondent for the *Toronto Star Weekly,* he covered the Greco-Turkish war and the conferences in Geneva and Lausanne. He had written some stories by that time but his wife, Hadley, lost the valise containing all of them on her way to Lausanne where she wanted to join her husband. This proved a blessing in disguise for it made Hemingway begin again, concentrate and rewrite as advised by Gertrude Stein.

In 1923 Hemingway travelled to Spain to see bullfights for the first time. This was the beginning of a lifelong affair with Spain and bullfights. 1923 saw the publication of his first book, *Three Stories and Ten Poems* (Contact Editions), and the birth of his first child, John Hadley "Bumby" Nicanor Hemingway, endearingly referred to as "Bumby" in Toronto.

The Hemingways returned to Paris from Toronto in 1924, and Hemingway joined Ford Madox Ford's *Transatlantic Review* as Associate Editor. His literary circle was much larger now and he started getting noticed as a writer.

Boni and Liveright published Hemingway's first major work, *In our Time*, in 1925, on Sherwood Anderson's recommendation. Hemingway met Pauline Pfeiffer, a staffer of the Paris edition of *Vogue,* whom he was to marry two years later, and Scott Fitzgerald, with whom he developed a close friendship. He visited Pamplona with family and friends in the same year and got the inspiration and material for his novel, *The Sun Also Rises*.

The success of *In our Time* gave him a self-confidence, which prompted him to declare his literary independence by parodying the style of Sherwood Anderson in *The Torrents of Spring* and sending it to Boni and Liveright for publication. Boni and Liveright rejected the manuscript as it made fun of their leading author. The rejection nullified the contract and freed Hemingway to seek another publisher. Charles Scribner's Sons published it and his next novel, *The Sun Also Rises*, in 1926, and all of his subsequent works.

Hemingway divorced Hadley Richardson and married Pauline Pfeiffer in May 1927. He published *Men without Women* in the same year. In 1928, he started writing *A Farewell to Arms*, based on his experiences as a Red Cross Ambulance Driver in Italy wounded at Fossalta. The birth of his second son, Patrick, by Caesarian section supplied the material for the conclusion of this novel, which was to be published in 1929. In 1928, he moved to Keywest, Florida, and began ocean-fishing. His father committed suicide in December 1928 as he himself was to do thirty-three years later.

Hemingway met with a car accident in October 1930 and spent eight weeks in a hospital in Billings, Montana. Pauline's uncle bought the Keywest home as a gift for her in 1931. Hemingway's third son, Gregory Hancock Hemingway, was born in November of the same year.

His *Death in the Afternoon*, a treatise on bullfighting, which includes his views on the craft of writing and his aesthetic principles, was published in 1932. He began marlin-fishing in the same year and caught fifty marlin in two months in 1933. He published his third collection of short stories, *Winner Take Nothing,* in 1933 and went on an African Safari with Pauline in the same year.

In 1935, Hemingway published *Green Hills of Africa*, a fictionalized account of his African Safari. 1936 saw the publication of two of his most anthologized stories, "The Snows of Kilimanjaro" and "The Short Happy Life of Francis Macomber."

He went to Spain in 1937 as a war correspondent to cover the Spanish Civil War for the North Atlantic Newspapers Association (NANA). He published his third novel, *To Have and Have Not* and his only play, *The Fifth Column*. In 1940 he divorced Pauline and married Martha Gellhorn, a fellow journalist, whom he had met in Spain. He also published *For Whom the Bell Tolls*, a novel based on the Spanish Civil War. He visited China with Martha in 1941.

Hemingway made Havana (Cuba) his home where he lived in *Finca Vigia* ('Look Out Farm'), and patrolled the North coast of Cuba in his fishing boat, "Pilar", looking for Nazi submarines in 1942, with the approval of the Government of the U.S.A., at the height of the Second World War.

In 1944 he went to England and Europe as war correspondent for Collier's to cover the Second World War with the Fourth Infantry of the Army of the U.S.A. In London, he met Mary Welsh, who was writing for the London Bureau of *Time*, *Life*, and *Fortune* magazines. He divorced Martha and married Mary in March 1946. He was working off and on on *Islands in the Stream*, and *The Garden of Eden* during this period.

In 1945 he travelled in Italy, where, in Venice, he met the beautiful Adriana Ivancich, who inspired *Across the River and into the Trees* and the character, Renata. This novel, of which Hemingway thought very highly, was published in 1950. The novel was adversely reviewed, which upset Hemingway whose health was already in a bad shape at this time.

The publication of *The Old Man and the Sea* in *Life* magazine in 1952 saw a sudden spurt in his fortunes. He won the Pulitzer Prize in 1953 and travelled to Spain, a country he loved much, to watch the bullfights which he missed for two decades. In January 1954 he went with Mary on an African Safari (his second African Safari), and suffered two air crashes in quick succession. They were believed to be dead and he had the unique privilege of knowing what the world thought of him as a man and a writer by reading the obituaries and tributes in the newspapers and magazines. It was in Lake

Victoria Hotel at Entebbe, Uganda, where he read them with great pleasure and amusement. His injuries included a full-scale concussion, a ruptured liver, spleen and kidney, temporary loss of vision in the left eye, loss of hearing in the left ear, a crushed vertebra, a sprained right arm and shoulder, a sprained left leg, and bad burns on his face, arms and head. Lying in his bed, he told newsmen that he had never been better.

It was widely believed that he would be awarded the Nobel Prize for literature in 1954. A few months later, he was awarded the Nobel Prize. He could not attend the Awards Ceremony in Stockholm and sent an acceptance message. In 1955 and 1956 he assisted in filming *The Old Man and the Sea*.

Hemingway's *The Dangerous Summer*, a non-fiction account of a bullfighting "duel" was serialized in *Life* magazine in 1960. He suffered from depression, delusions and paranoia and was admitted to the Mayo Clinic in Rochester, Minnesota, where he was given electric shock therapy. He had been living in Ketchum, Idaho, during that time. In 1961 he was discharged from Mayo Clinic and returned to Ketchum, but had to be readmitted there owing to suicidal depression. After two months he returned to Ketchum and killed himself with his shotgun on July 2, 1961.

A *Moveable Feast* (1964), *Islands in the Stream* (1970), *The Garden of Eden* (1986), and *True at First Light* (1999) were all published posthumously. There is still a lot of unpublished material in the Hemingway Room of the John F. Kennedy Presidential Library in Boston and it will not be a surprise if more posthumous works are published in future.

Apart from his image as a legendary writer, Hemingway cultivated a He-Man image which made him a legend in his lifetime. Part of it was inherited from his father and the other part was either thrust upon him by circumstances or cultivated by him to overcome certain psychological problems. He was a very impressive looking man. Carlos Baker describes him thus:

> One's first impression of him was of size and strength. He was six feet tall and usually weighed about 210

> pounds. He had a tendency to put on weight and was once up to 260 pounds. His eyes were brown, his complexion ruddy and there were dimples in both his cheeks which his beard later concealed... *(Ernest Hemingway: A Life Story*, 3-4).

He loved outdoor activities and manly sports. Fishing and bullfighting were the two great passions of his life; boxing and big-game-hunting came next. He loved war and violence and reported on the Greco-Turkish War, the Spanish Civil War, and the Second World War. He was a Red Cross Ambulance Driver in the Italian army and was severely wounded and later decorated by the Army. The wound left a permanent scar on his psyche and influenced his life and writing in a remarkable way. He sought danger and took the gravest of risks trying to look death in the face again and again, which is called "Repetitive Compulsion" in psychological terms. All the protagonists in his novels are wounded or scarred in some way or the other.

Hemingway's primary concern was the aesthetics of truthful writing and the problem of depiction. He says in *Death in the Afternoon*:

> ... I found the greatest difficulty, aside from knowing truly what you really felt, rather than what you were supposed to feel, and had been taught to feel, was to put down what really happened in action; what the actual things were which produced the emotion that you experienced (10).

With this objective in view, Hemingway started with the simplest things, "and one of the simplest things of all and the most fundamental is violent death" (10). He went to Spain to study life and death reduced to their simplest form in the bull-ring. Hemingway's aesthetic faith, like Thoreau's, is a faith in the power of simplicity. This is reflected in his narration, description, characterization, and dialogue. His writing shows how old simple words can be charged with a new power. His mastery of narration and language has earned for him a permanent place among the great writers of the world.

2

Formative Influences

Hemingway was sixteen years old when he started writing seriously. Miss Fanny Biggs and Miss Margaret Dixon, teachers in the Oak Park High School, where he was studying, discovered the writer in him. An older student, who saw a good deal of him in 1915-16, testifies thus according to Charles Fenton:

> He had a typewriter on the third floor, well away from his family. By that time he was writing for the fun of it and apparently felt that he was developing ability along that line. He would read to me some of the things he was writing and was quite enthusiastic (17).

His first published story, "Judgment of Manitou" appeared in *Tabula*, the school literary magazine, in February 1916. It was a very readable story revealing the young author's interest in the mechanics of the narrative art and his early absorption in the theme of violence.

It was followed by "A Matter of Colour" in the same year in the April issue of the *Tabula*. It was an ironic story about a crooked fight with a 'wow' at the end in the O. Henry fashion. The narration was in the form of a monologue by a fight manager with occasional dialogue, and the language was an attempt to bring out the authentic idiom.

"Sepi Jingan" appeared in the November 1916 issue of the *Tabula*. It was an improvement over the two earlier stories and showed that the writer was conscious of his narrative technique. The story is about an Indian killer who is presented as an interesting character embodying good and bad at once. Though a killer, he had a likeable side to his character. The dialogue, with its repetitive rhythms, reminds us, at places, of the later Hemingway:

> Yes. He was a bad Indian. Up on the upper peninsula, he couldn't get drunk. He used to drink all day—everything. But he couldn't get drunk. Then he would get crazy; but he wasn't drunk. He was crazy because he couldn't get drunk (Fenton, 26).

Look at the following passage put in the mouth of a similar character ten years later in one of Hemingway's well-known stories:

> Right away I liked him and when I got out I looked him up. He likes to think I'm crazy and I don't mind. I like to be with him and I like seeing the country and I don't have to commit no larceny to do it. I like living like a gentleman (*In our Time*, 77-78).

The technique of making the character, whose vocabulary is very limited, have recourse to repetition of words, especially simple verbs like "get drunk" or "like" to make him sound natural seems to have appealed to the young school boy writing his first exercises in the craft of fiction.

His by-line became an almost regular feature in *The Trapeze*, the weekly paper of the school. Arthur Bobbit, then in-charge of the paper, gave him the assignment. Ring Lardner was the most popular writer in the Chicago area at that time, and Hemingway imitated him in *The Trapeze* under the caption, "Ring Lardner Returns." This was an excellent early training for Hemingway in writing effective prose, and he did not forget his early admiration for Ring Lardner. Years later, when, as a celebrated writer, he autographed a book for Ring Lardner, he wrote, "To Ring Lardner from his early imitator and always admirer, Ernest Hemingway" (Fenton, 31).

JOURNALISM

Hemingway's association with the *Kansas City Star* for seven months in 1917 served as his apprenticeship in writing. The *Star* provided good training to its reporters and inculcated in them a love and regard for writing.

They followed its famous style sheet containing 110 rules. When we look at some of these rules we can understand how Hemingway profited from them:

> Use short sentences. Use short first paragraphs. Use vigorous English. Be positive, not negative, ... Never use old slang. Such words as *stunt*, *cut out*, *get his goat*, *come across*, *sit up and take notice*, *put one over*; ... have no place after their use becomes common. Slang to be enjoyable must be fresh; ... Avoid the use of adjectives, especially such extravagant ones as *splendid*, *gorgeous*, *grand*, *magnificent*, etc. (Fenton, 35-37).

Hemingway is reported to have told Paul W. Fisher, in an interview published in *Kansas City Times* on 26th November 1940, that these were the best rules he ever learned for the business of writing: "I've never forgotten them. No man with any talent, who feels and writes truly about the thing he is trying to say, can fail to write well if he abides by them" (Fenton, 37). Hemingway's declarative sentences and his avoidance of hackneyed adjectives and literary flourishes could be traced to his training in the office of the *Kansas City Star* and his association with men like C.G. Wellington (Pete Wellington) and Lionel Calhoun Moise.

Even as an ambulance driver during the Austro-Italian war he did not give up writing. His "Al Receives Another Letter", written in the style of Ring Lardner, was the longest single item of the June 1918 issue of *Ciao*, brought out by Section IV of the Ambulance Corps.

His experiences on the Italian front including his serious injury at *Fossalta di Piave*, were an important part of his apprenticeship as a writer. The traumatic shock, leading to a kind of obsessive interest in and preoccupation with the violent side of life and death in his writings, and the 'repetitive compulsion', of which Philip Young speaks in his book-length study of Hemingway, are explained to a large extent by these experiences. They also provided ample material for his future fictional endeavour, and one of his major novels, *A Farewell to Arms*, of which the present work is a critical study, was a direct result of his Italian experiences during the Austro-Italian war. It was his 'baptism of fire'—to use a common phrase of the times—in every sense of the term and gave him a new outlook on life and an essential humility and sympathetic understanding of things, which were generally concealed by a rough exterior. On December 21, 1926, he wrote to Maxwell Perkins that he had "not been at all hard boiled since 8th July, 1918—on the night of which I discovered that that was also vanity" (Baker, *Selected Letters*, 4). This shows the impact of his injury on his future writing which deals with the theme of the vanity of all human endeavour.

When he returned home after a dozen operations, cane in hand and with a slight limp, he was lionized as a war-hero, but soon felt disenchanted with Oak Park. He went up to Northern Michigan where he pursued his favourite occupations of fishing and writing during the summer. He worked hard but could not sell his writing. But his stay in Michigan gave him material for much of his early fiction beginning with the story, "Up in Michigan". After the summer he joined the Toronto *Star Weekly* and the *Daily Star*, and was an active journalist for four years. J. Herbert Cranston, editor of the *Star Weekly,* recognized Hemingway's talent and encouraged him by publishing whatever he wrote. As the *Star Weekly* laid more emphasis on entertainment than information, Hemingway felt encouraged to experiment with satire, parody, and irony, which he was to use with great skill in his major fiction. Gregory Clerk, the feature editor of the *Star Weekly,* said in 1952: "His use of words was precise, aware. His diction—his choice of words, I mean—was extraordinary" (Fenton, 74), while Cranston, the editor, called him "a born writer" (Fenton, 80).

The winter of 1920 saw him as an associate editor of *Cooperative Commonwealth*. He lived in Y.K. Smith's apartment, where he met Kate, Smith's sister, who was to marry John Dos Passos later, her friend, Edith Foley, a free-lance writer, and Donald M. Wright, an advertising man. They were all interested in art and literature. Hemingway was the hardest working of the lot: "In the evenings when the others were idling in the living room, Hemingway was apt to be in the room, typing" (Fenton, 87).

Sherwood Anderson, who was already a famous writer, visited them often as a friend of Smith and Wright's. He was impressed with Hemingway in no time and said to his hosts: "Thanks for introducing me to that young fellow. I think he's going to go some place."

Hemingway was not impressed with Anderson's concept of unconscious art and narrative style. Though it was widely believed that Anderson's work had influenced Hemingway's, Anderson himself never said so. There is no doubt that Hemingway respected Anderson, who introduced him to Gertrude Stein and others in Paris and helped him get his first book published. In his letter of May 21, 1926, explaining *The Torrents of Spring* to Anderson, he says that if Anderson, who could write great things, published something that seemed to him (Hemingway) rotten, the writer (Anderson) should be told, and that if some writer produces slop and gets applause, America will never produce any truly great writers (White, 263).

Hemingway worked at his craft with tremendous intensity and conviction. He once told Donald Wright at Smith's apartment: "You've got to see it, feel it, smell it, hear it", and as he sat in the gym waiting to get in the ring, he would try to identify the various smells and record the sensations afterwards (Fenton, 88).

During this period he married Hadley Richardson and the young couple were anxious to go to Europe and it became possible when Hemingway became the roving correspondent for the *Star* based in Paris. This suited Hemingway very well as it not only gave him the freedom to pursue the craft of fiction but also gave him the opportunity of living and working in the creative atmosphere of Paris.

PARIS

Sherwood Anderson had just returned from Paris and its cultural and literary ambience and the Hemingways left for Paris armed with letters of introduction from Anderson.

As a roving correspondent, he had the opportunity of travelling widely, observing men and manners, and covering the famous Lousanne conference. The job not only helped the Hemingways make both ends meet for four years but also enriched his understanding of things and gave him much material for his *Star* stories and his future creative work. His newspaper work was a good exercise for him in the craft of writing. Apart from the art of dramatizing a story, his technique of translating rhythm from one language into another, which he later used with much success in his major fiction set in foreign countries like Spain, France, Italy and Cuba, and his technique of wrapping up irony in humour or concealing it in some situation or dialogue can be seen in many of these newspaper stories. The following passage in which a demobbed soldier explains his domestic difficulties to another is a good example for rendering the foreign idiom:

> It is my wife's system. She goes into the shoe shop and says, "I want a pair of shoes for *mon mari*. Not expensive. Mon mari's feet are this much longer than mine, I believe, and this much wider. That will do nicely. Wrap them up." Old one, it is terrible! (*The Wild Years: Ernest Hemingway*, ed. Gene Z. Hanrahan, 84)

For irony in the guise of a humorous situation, the story of the post man, who must be tipped, is a good example. After delivering a letter, he is overwhelmed by the unexpectedly large tip:

> "Senor", says the postman, "I am an honest man. Your generosity has touched my heart. Here is another letter. I had intended to save it for tomorrow to ensure another reward from the always generous Senor. But here it is, Let us hope that it will be as splendid a letter as the first" (Hanrahan, 168).

His eye for the dramatic moment and the *mot juste* reveals itself in this sentence in which he describes that all the chairs except those of the Soviet delegation were filled at the Geneva Conference: "The hall is crowded and sweltering and the four empty chairs of the Soviet delegation are the four emptiest looking chairs I have ever seen" (Hanrahan, 176).

Paris was the cradle of art and letters, a school for aspiring writers and artists, and Hemingway made the best use of his life in Paris, subjecting himself to hard discipline in the school of Gustave Flaubert. His apprentice work in fiction was submitted to the scrutiny of Gertrude Stein and Ezra Pound. His stories came back from Pound, blue-pencilled, with most of the adjectives gone and with unsparing comments.

Gertrude Stein was full of new ideas about writing and was experimenting with prose-writing. She paid special attention to 'repetition' and used it with considerable skill.

Hemingway was impressed with her efforts to give a new dimension to English prose. By copying her manuscript of *The Making of Americans* and correcting the proofs, he not only helped Stein but studied her method thoroughly. She read everything Hemingway had written up to that point, liked the poems, but found the unfinished novel wanting, with a great deal of "not particularly good description" and advised him to "begin over again and concentrate" (Fenton, 119). John Peale Bishop reports that Hemingway said to him: "Ezra was right half the time and when he was wrong, he was so wrong you were never in any doubt about it. Gertrude was always right" (152).

Sylvia Beach's excellent bookshop in Paris, "Shakespeare and Company", was of immense use to Hemingway. Here, he went through an intensive course in reading prose-masters like Turgenev, Chekhov, Tolstoy, Dostoevski, Stendhal, Balzac, Flaubert, and James Joyce. Besides, it was in this bookshop that young Hemingway occasionally met distinguished writers like T.S. Eliot and James Joyce.

Hemingway learnt much from painting and music too. He told Lillian Ross in the *New Yorker* interview:

> I learnt to write by looking at paintings in the Luxembourg Museum in Paris.... I can make a landscape like Mr. Paul Cezanne. I learned how to make a landscape from Mr. Paul Cezanne by walking through the Luxembourg

> Museum a thousand times with an empty gut, and I am pretty sure that if Mr. Paul was around, he would like the way I make them and be happy that I learned it from him (35-36).

He says in *A Moveable Feast*:

> I was learning something from the painting of Cezanne that made writing simple true sentences far from enough to make the stories have the dimensions that I was trying to put in them. I was learning very much from him but I was not articulate enough to explain it to anyone. Besides, it was a secret (17-18).

He learned from music, especially from Bach. He told Lillian Ross how Bach helped him in writing the first paragraphs of *A Farewell to Arms*:

> In the first paragraph of 'Farewell' [sic], I used the word 'and' consciously over and over the way Mr. Johann Sebastian Bach used a note in music when he was emitting counterpoint. I can almost write like Mr. Johann sometimes—or, anyway, so he would like it. All such people are easy to deal with, because we all know you have to learn (36).

It cannot be said that he learnt only from Stein, Pound, Cezanne, and Bach. He kept his eyes and ears and, above all, his mind open, and learnt from all his experiences, from his discussions with the writers he moved with, like John Dos Passos, Malcolm Cowley, Archibald Macleish, James Joyce, Ford Madox Ford, William Carlos Williams, and Scott Fitzgerald, with artists like Henry Strater and Waldo Pierce, and with correspondents like Guy Hickok, Lincoln Steffens, William Bird, W.B. Ryall, and Sisley Huddleston.

Sylvia Beach, who saw him on a daily basis in her bookshop during his stay in Paris, pays him this tribute in *Shakespeare and Company*:

> Hemingway was a widely educated young man, who knew many countries and several languages; and he had learnt it all at first hand, not in universities. He seemed

> to me to have gone a great deal farther and faster than any of the young writers I knew. In spite of a certain boyishness, he was exceptionally wise and self-reliant (88).

A good writer values tradition so much that he uses his knowledge of classics to make a new classic. It is not necessary to discard one's tradition to be a modern. Therefore, Gertrude Stein's remark that Hemingway looks like a modern but smells of the museums is unfair.

The influence of many of his predecessors and contemporaries can be traced in his work as in T.S. Eliot's work. Some of them are Mark Twain, who was the first man to write 'American' really well; Stephen Crane, who was himself influenced by Twain; Turgenev, who, with his simplicity, brevity, and intensity, gives the sense of a physical background in fiction; Sherwood Anderson, whose Winesburg, Ohio, Hemingway acknowledged as his first pattern in a discussion with Dean Christian Gauss and Scott Fitzgerald; Gustave Flaubert, in whose discipline he learned his craft under the guidance of Ezra Pound and Gertrude Stein; James Joyce, whom he greatly admired and whose *Ulysses* he helped smuggle into the U.S.A.; and T.S. Eliot, from whom he claims to have learned to play with quotations and with whom he largely shares the theory of objective correlative, which he applies to prose.

These influences point to the hard way Hemingway cultivated his craft, but dwindle into insignificance when we are involved with Hemingway at his best.

A very important influence on his prose style is *The Bible*. One of the supplementary textbooks in his Oak Park High School was Rhodes's *Old Testament Narratives*. He told Samuel Putnam in an interview that took place in Paris shortly after the publication of *The Sun Also Rises* in 1925 that he learnt to write by reading the *Bible*, adding that by the *Bible* he meant particularly *The Old Testament* (Fenton, 16).

A writer's experiences in life, in his formative years as well as in his later years when he comes to grips with life and its problems, form part of his creative equipment. Hemingway's experiences were transmuted into artistic forms by the alchemy of his art. He is one of those rare craftsmen who consciously subject themselves to long years of apprenticeship and hard work undergoing poverty and privation in order to learn and master the technique of his trade.

3

The Hemingway Aesthetic

Hemingway was awarded the Nobel Prize for Literature "for his powerful style-making mastery of the art of modern narration" and the citation further described him as "one of those who, honestly and undauntedly, reproduces the genuine features of the hard countenance of the age." He did not attend the ceremonies in Stockholm on December 10, 1954, and sent an acceptance message which was read by the U.S. Ambassador, Mr. John C. Cabot. This message presents Hemingway's aesthetics in a nutshell. His aesthetic opinions are expressed mostly in *Death in the Afternoon* and *Green Hills of Africa*, in his introduction to *Men at War*, and in his casual remarks in the course of his articles, conversations, and interviews. But in his Nobel Prize acceptance speech, he epitomizes all his earlier pronouncements on literature and art and presents his literary credo in two hundred and six words with his characteristic verbal economy:

> ... Things may not be immediately discernible in what a man writes, and in this sometimes he is fortunate; but eventually they are quite clear and by these and the degree of alchemy that he possesses he will endure or be forgotten.
>
> Writing, at its best, is a lonely life. Organizations for writers palliate the writer's loneliness but I doubt if they improve his writing. He grows in public stature as he sheds his loneliness and often his work deteriorates. For he does his work alone and if he is a good enough writer he must face eternity, or the lack of it, each day.

> For a true writer each book should be a new beginning where he tries again for something that is beyond attainment. He should always try for something that has never been done or that others have tried and failed. Then sometimes, with great luck, he will succeed.
>
> How simple the writing of literature would be if it were only necessary to write in another way what has been well written. It is because we have had such great writers in the past that a writer is driven far out past where he can go, out to where no one can help him (Carlos Baker, *Ernest Hemingway: The Writer as Artist*, 339).

Hemingway believes that writing at its best is a lonely life: "For he does his work alone and if he is a good enough writer he must face eternity or the lack of it, each day." This underlines the need for truthfulness. Once he sheds his aesthetic loneliness and becomes part of the crowd, he will feel and write what he is supposed to feel and write. The result will be insincere writing, and his work deteriorates. The true, committed writer, being lonely, is answerable to himself, and any deviation from the truth would amount to self-deception. Since the writer is concerned with rendition of experience and emotion, he must take care to kindle the intended emotion in the reader. This requires the writer to pinpoint the actual things which produce the emotion. Hemingway explains it thus in *Death in the Afternoon*:

> I was trying to write then and I found the greatest difficulty, aside from knowing truly what you really felt, rather than what you were supposed to feel, was to put down what really happened in action; what the actual things were which produced the emotion that you experienced.... and one of the simplest things of all and the most fundamental is violent death (10).

Violent death is one of the simplest things in the world because it is free from the complications of natural death. When Hemingway tells us how he went to Spain to study life and death reduced to their simplest form in the bullring, he sounds like Thoreau explaining how he went to Walden and reduced life to its simplest terms in order to "front only the essential facts of life" and "learn what it had to teach". His aesthetic faith like Thoreau's, is a faith in simplicity. This simplicity is reflected in his narration, description, characterization and dialogue. To achieve this simplicity in his fiction, he mastered the technique of verbal economy—the art of using a few telling words instead of writing a great deal.

Hemingway's insistence on what you really felt, rather than what you were supposed to feel needs a little elucidation. The reader wants the right feeling and emotion, but not the writer's feeling and emotion. Hence, he must watch out and avoid all irrelevant feelings and learn to find out what he really feels and separate it from what he is supposed to feel, what he wants to feel etc. If he is unable to do it, he will fall into namby-pambyism and will fail to produce the feeling the action or object he describes really evokes. True objectivity can be achieved only when the mind is cleansed of all irrelevant emotions and preconceptions preparatory to receiving the right emotion.

In his introduction to *Men at War*, Hemingway says that a writer should be of as great probity and honesty as a priest of God and is either chaste or not as a woman is either chaste or not:

> A writer's job is to tell the truth. His standard of fidelity to the truth should be so high that his invention, out of his experience, should produce a truer account than anything factual can be. For facts can be observed badly; but when a good writer is creating something, he has time and scope to make it of an absolute truth (xv).

Guided by this aesthetic principle of truth, Hemingway followed the kinetographic technique in much of his writing, particularly the vignettes in *In our Time*:

> If it happened right down close in front of you, you could see Villalta snarl at the bull and curse him, and when the bull charged he swung back firmly like an oak when the wind hits it, his legs tight together, the muleta trailing and the sword following the curve behind. Then

> he cursed the bull, flopped the muleta at him, and swung back from the charge, his feet firm, and muleta curving and at each swing the crowd roaring (137).

Hemingway continued to use this technique in his later work too. Look at this passage from *A Farewell to Arms*, in which a scene in the operation theatre is recorded from the outside:

> I thought Catherine was dead. She looked dead. Her face was grey, the part of it that I could see. Down below, under the light, the doctor was sewing up the great long, forcep-spread, thick-edged wound. Another doctor in a mask gave the anaesthetic. Two nurses in masks handed things. It looked like a drawing of the Inquisition (250).

Hemingway must have realized that a rigorous practice of this technique might cause the recording of action from the outside resulting in distortion of facts for there is a brilliant departure from this method in the fourteenth sketch of *In our Time* in which the death of Maera is described:

> Maera lay still, his head on his arms, his face in the sand. He felt warm and sticky from the bleeding.... Maera wanted to say something and found he could not talk. Maera felt everything getting larger and larger and then smaller and smaller. Then everything commenced to run faster as when they speed up a cinematograph film. Then he was dead (175).

Here the writer enters the consciousness of Maera and describes things from Maera's viewpoint. It is a recording of sensations from inside. Hemingway transcends the kinetographic method here.

The reference to cinematograph film in the above vignette strengthens Earl Rovit's view that Hemingway could have been influenced by D.W. Griffith's pioneer application of movie-camera close-ups (45).

One of Hemingway's strong points is his freedom from the writer's weakness of intruding into his fictional world either to make profound utterances himself or to make his characters do so. He keeps his eye unblinkingly on the action and the emotion generated, and does not allow the intellect to interfere. He says in *Death in the Afternoon*:

> When writing a novel, a writer should create living people; people not characters. A *character* is a caricature. If a writer can make people live, there may be no great characters in his book, but it is possible that his book will remain as a whole; as an entity; as a novel. If the people the writer is making talk of old masters; of music; of painting; of letters; or of science then they should talk of those subjects in the novel. If they do not talk of those subjects and the writer makes them talk of them he is a faker, and if he talks about them himself to show how much he knows, then he is showing off. No matter how good a phrase or a simile he may have if he puts it in where it is not absolutely necessary and irreplaceable, he is spoiling his work for egotism. Prose is architecture, not interior decoration, and the Baroque is over (182).

It is clear from the above passage that Hemingway values compactness and unity of effect in a work of art rather than characterization. It is the creation of a world of living people that is important rather than artificially made characters which are no better than caricatures.

His truthful and objective depiction of experience made him cultivate a style shorn of ornament and unnecessary detail. Even when he expresses his aesthetic ideas he avoids literary jargon. Joseph Warren Beach compares his work to the furniture that came into vogue on the continent during that period—"great masses of wood uncarved and unmodified by fluted pilasters and brasses and curlicues—with straight metal pipes in place of curved and claw-footed legs, and the fewest possible pieces in any one room" (100).

Intellectual and emotional honesty and steadfast truthfulness should be the guiding principle of a writer since he does his work alone and must face eternity.

THINGS NOT IMMEDIATELY DISCERNIBLE

"Things may not be immediately discernible in what a man writes, ... and by these and a degree of alchemy that he possesses, he will endure or be forgotten."

Hemingway believes that if a writer knows what he is writing about and is writing truly enough, he may omit things that he knows and the reader will have a feeling of those things as strongly as though the writer had stated them. He says in *Death in the Afternoon*, "The dignity of movement of an iceberg is due to only one-eighth of it being above water" (183). He tells us in *A Moveable Feast* that he had omitted the real ending of the story, "Out of Season", which was that the old man hanged himself, in accordance with this theory (69). Illustrating this aesthetic principle to George Plimpton, he explains how he omitted everything unnecessary to conveying the experience to the reader in *The Old Man and the Sea*, which could have been over a thousand pages long:

> I've seen the marlin mate and know about that. So I leave that out. I've seen a school (or pod) of more than fifty sperm whales in that same stretch of water and once harpooned one nearly sixty feet in length and lost him. So I left that out. All the stories I know from the fishing village I leave out. But the knowledge is what makes the underwater part of the iceberg (34-35).

This attitude reflects the influence of impressionist painters, chiefly Cezanne, on Hemingway. At the Impressionist Museum in Paris he showed a Cezanne to Hotchner and said that it had been his life's ambition to write "as good as that picture". Hotchner quotes Hemingway's words: "Haven't made it yet, but getting closer all the time ... artists have all those great colours, while I have to do it on the typewriter or with my pencil in black and white" (187).

The Iceberg Theory operates in the same way as the theory of 'suggestion' in literary criticism which Horace calls the "elbows of action" in *Ars Poetica* and the theory of *Dhvani* in Sanskrit poetics. It operates at the different levels of depiction and dialogue. It is the writer's economy of expression by impression through suppression. Here Hemingway's method is very much like T.S. Eliot's objective correlative. Like Eliot, Hemingway concentrates on the actual things which produce the emotion. Six years before Hemingway published his first important book, T.S. Eliot had published his famous essay: "Hamlet and His Problems" (1919) in which he propounded the theory of "objective correlative"—a set of objects, a situation, a chain of events or a quotation "which shall be the formula of that particular emotion" (100).

Hemingway evokes an emotional awareness in the reader by a highly suggestive pictorial detail, and has done for prose what Eliot has done for poetry. His own observation on Eliot's theory in "Hamlet and His Problems" and his parallel passage about the iceberg in *Death in the Afternoon* is reported to be: "Mr. Eliot works his side of the street and I work mine" (Welland, 21).

It is interesting to see how Hemingway has perfected a technique which is all right in poetry, but extremely difficult to use in prose narrative:

> They shot the six cabinet ministers at half past six in the morning against the wall of a hospital. There were pools of water in the courtyard. There were wet dead leaves on the paving of the courtyard. It rained hard. All the shutters of the hospital were nailed shut. One of the ministers was sick with typhoid. Two soldiers carried him downstairs and out into the rain. They tried to hold him up against the wall but he sat down in a puddle of water. The other five stood very quietly against the wall. Finally the officer told the soldiers it was no good trying to make him stand up. When they fired the first volley he was sitting down in the water with his head on his knees (*In our Time*, 63).

The writer makes no comment, expresses no emotion. It is a cool, objective recording in a flat tone, which looks like a kinetographic reproduction of action. But the suggestive details are there for the discerning reader—the pools of water which will soon turn into pools of blood in the courtyard, the wet 'dead' leaves, the rain which is a sign of disaster, the shutters of the hospital, the place of healing and health, being nailed shut and the sick minister sitting in a puddle of water. Such emotive details would surely give the reader a moving mental picture of the tragic scene and give him the right emotion without the writer injecting his emotions into the reader's mind. The cabinet ministers are killed against the wall of a hospital, which is a place where they try to save lives. Therefore, it is appropriate that the shutters of the hospital windows are nailed shut. The verb, 'nailed' evokes the image of crucifixion, which is repeated against the hospital walls. The sick minister sits in a 'puddle' of water. The dull, heavy word 'puddle', which shows how the sick man slumped down, is used instead of the ordinary 'pool'. By thus using dramatic and emotive correlatives, the writer makes the reader actively participate in the narrative.

T.S. Eliot's usual practice is to make use of complex literary symbols as objective correlatives in order to evoke a controlled emotional response. A certain standard of literary and cultural background is necessary to appreciate these symbols in Eliot. For example, when we read the line "Those are pearls that were his eyes" in *The Waste Land*, we should be reminded of the same line in Ariel's song in Shakespeare's *The Tempest,* appreciate the situation of Ferdinand who thinks that he has lost his father, come back to the *The Waste Land*, and examine the context before we become capable of a completely satisfying response. Though Hemingway's medium is prose-narrative which is bound to be more lucid, and less abstruse and complex than poetry, he is also found to be doing certain interesting things with his images and with suggestive words under the surface of his narrative as the following passage from *In our Time* illustrates:

> We were in a garden in Mons. Young Buckley came in with his patrol from across the river. The first German I saw climbed up over the garden wall. We waited till he got one leg over and then potted him. He had so much equipment on and looked awfully surprised and fell down, into the garden. Then three more came over

> further down the wall. We shot them. They all came just like that (33).

The above narrative of how the speaker and his friends killed the attacking Germans is, on the surface, a kinetographic reproduction of action with no reference to the narrator's emotions. The discerning reader, however, will find the use of the verb 'potted' suggestive, with its aspirated 'p' coming abruptly after the long unit of thought ("The first German I saw climbed up over the garden wall. We waited till he got one leg over and then"), which suggests the difficulty the German had in climbing up the wall and the snipers' breathless waiting before potting him. The look of surprise on the face of the German with "so much equipment on" is really pathetic in that it reveals that he is *not equipped* with the knowledge of the ambush. All this happens in a garden. A sensitive reader who reads between the lines, will find the garden as the objective correlative for the sin of man and the fruits thereof. The garden is the Garden of Eden from which man is expelled, and the expulsion is followed by the murder of brother by brother. The writer makes the garden the scene of action with an artistic motive, evoking the required mood and emotion. The objective correlative is neither far-fetched nor literary. It is a common garden even as it is a common hospital with its shutters nailed shut in the sketch about the six cabinet ministers. Hemingway takes his objective correlative from observed reality and common experience.

The 'Iceberg' principle is also illustrated by the clipped dialogue with its undertones of things left unsaid and the tight-lipped conclusions of his stories. The alchemy referred to in Hemingway's acceptance message consists in his technique, his treatment of his subject that will make him endure.

TRYING FOR SOMETHING BEYOND ATTAINMENT

Hemingway believes that for a true writer each book should be a new beginning where he tries again for something beyond attainment. This attempt to do something beyond attainment is an essentially romantic approach and is characteristic of the American "romance" tradition which is

Hemingway's literary heritage. Hemingway uses the word "classic" significantly in *Green Hills of Africa*:

> A new classic does not bear any resemblance to the classics that have preceded it. It can steal from anything that it is better than, anything that is not classic, all classics do that. Some writers are born only to help another writer to write one sentence. But it cannot derive from or resemble a previous classic (21).

Any writer who achieves a degree of permanence is a classic. A new classic may borrow from an inferior work, but, at the same time, may not bear any resemblance to that work or to the preceding classics, since each book is a new beginning where the writer tries for something beyond attainment, going "far out past where he can go, out to where no one can help him" like an Ahab or a Santiago. Every literary effort is a new challenge to a writer who wishes to last, and a real work of art lasts forever. Hemingway declares in *Green Hills of Africa*:

> A country, finally, erodes and the dust blows away, the people all die and none of them were of any importance permanently, except those who practiced the arts, ... A thousand years makes economics silly and a work of art endures forever, but it is very difficult to do and now it is not fashionable (109).

Hemingway's writing has many classical virtues. His clear, objective observation of what really happens in action, stripping away what is not absolutely necessary, his concentration on the significant emotive details, his avoidance of exuberant and rhetorical writing, and his deliberate suppression of certain details for effect, point to his classical bent of mind. But the fact that his creative imagination is anchored to his own experience, making his themes highly subjective and personal, and his belief that a new book should try for something beyond attainment make him a romantic.

He believes that art is a microcosmic representation of the universe, and the important thing is to make a true work of art. He says in *Death in the Afternoon*: "Let those who want to save the world if you can get to see it clear and as a whole.

Then any part you make will represent the whole if it's made truly" (261).

Hemingway's choice to work within certain limits has enabled him to achieve new depths in writing and explore the possibility of achieving new dimensions in prose.

4

Hemingway's Major Themes

The whole of Hemingway's work can be taken as a single unit. The general pattern of this is implicit in *In our Time* and is made explicit in the ironic juxtaposition between the two epigraphs prefacing his next important work, *The Sun Also Rises:*

> "You are all a lost generation."
> — Gertrude Stein in conversation.
> One generation passeth away, and another generation cometh: but the earth abideth forever .... The sun also ariseth, and the sun goeth down, and hasteth to his place where he arose... —*Ecclesiastes*.

The intervening novel, *The Torrents of Spring*, is ironically described on the title page as 'A Romantic Novel in honour of the passing of a Great Race'—the passing of a generation. Hemingway seems to be thinking of the pageant of passing generations against the vast background of the everlasting earth focusing the dialectic between the horological time and the geological time as Earl Rovit puts it, between the ephemeral and the eternal (126). He finds an objective correlative for this juxtaposition nine years later in the Gulf Stream which "has moved, as it moves, since before man" with the flotsam of palm-fronds, corks, bottles and electric light globes, condoms, and many other things as he puts it in *Greenhills of Africa*:

> ...the stream, with no visible flow, takes five loads of this a day when things are going well in La Habana and in ten miles along the coast, it is as clear and blue and unimpressed as it was ever before the tug hauled out the

> scow; and the palm-fronds of our victories, the worn light bulbs of our discoveries and the empty condoms of our great loves float with no significance against one single, lasting thing, the stream (148-150).

The Gulf Stream is the correlative image for the flux of life and the eternal earth. Counterpointed to it are a variety of human activities which have no effect on it. It goes on undisturbed around the little human drama on which interest is focused and which is like a drama in a theatre which has little effect on the life flowing outside.

This ironic theme is illustrated in all his fiction, major as well as minor, and becomes the main subject of *The Old Man and the Sea*, in which a man is pitted against the vast limitless ocean and its denizens. The first story of *In our Time*, "Indian camp", is sandwiched between two gloomy pageants. Chapter I, which precedes the story, describes a drunken battery going along the road while Chapter II, which follows the story, describes a gloomy procession of wartime evacuees herded along by Greek cavalry. Squeezed between these two processions is the poignant story of "The Indian camp" involving birth, death and pain. At the end of the story we find life flowing on normally.

The passage from *Green Hills of Africa* about the palm-fronds of our victories, the light bulbs of our discoveries, and the condoms of our love floating ineffectually on the Gulf Stream, makes us hark back to the epigraph from *The Ecclesiastes* prefacing *The Sun Also Rises* and the preacher's words preceding the epigraph:

> Vanity of vanities, saith the Preacher, vanity of vanities; all is vanity.
> What profit hath a man of all his labour which he taketh under the sun? (*Ecclesiastes*, 1: 2-3)

NADA, NIGHT AND DEATH

The awareness of the futility of all human endeavour is like a reflection of the "Slough of Despond" on the human mind. Night and death are its external symbols in the physical world. Hemingway calls this state of mind *nada* and makes it the subject of the story, "A Clean Well-Lighted Place", in which two waiters discuss with a man who has this awareness and the older waiter is conscious of this too and realizes that a clean well-lighted café affords temporary protection against *nada*. Ad of "The Battler" and Krebs of "Soldier's Home" are afflicted by *nada*. Nick of "A Way You'll Never Be" and "Big Two-Hearted River" leaves it behind but still dreads it. Nick finds a remedy for it in establishing contact with the concrete world— with the abiding earth and mother nature. He finds a therapeutic virtue in this Thoreauvian return to nature, which figures again in the Burguete episode in *The Sun Also Rises*. Glimpses of mother nature are there in the mountain country of the priest and in Frederick Henry and Catherine's escape to Switzerland in *A Farewell to Arms*.

The concrete manifestations of *nada* are night and death. Night plays an important role in the story, "Now I Lay Me", in which we find a man with a mortal dread of closing his eyes in the night. The theme recurs in *The Sun Also Rises* where Jake does not get sleep in the nights and in "A Clean Well-Lighted Place" in which the *nada*-affected waiter goes to sleep only at dawn.

Death is the night of life, and Hemingway is keenly interested in it, especially violent death. This is not only because of his early affair with it on the Italian war front, but also because of his desire to master his craft. Violent death implies pain and suffering which are present in all of Hemingway's fiction in some form or other, either physical or psychological.

COURAGE, SEX AND LOVE

A clean well-lighted place keeps off the advancing shadows of *nada*. In man, it is a stout heart with the courage to fight the good fight, the endurance to suffer pain without complaint, and the adherence to a certain code of conduct. It leads to victory in the face of defeat, converting material defeat into moral or spiritual triumph as in the case of Manuel Garcia, the forgotten old bullfighter in the story, "The Undefeated", or Frederic Henry in *A Farewell to Arms* or Santiago in *The Old*

Man and the Sea or Robert Jordan in *For Whom the Bell Tolls* or Jesus himself who "was pretty good in there", on the cross, in "Today Is Friday". Courage has a vital relevance to our situation. A man who lacks courage and is a slave to his fears is not truly free. As E.M. Halliday points out,

> In the image of the crucifixion, which has haunted Hemingway from "Today Is Friday" (1929) to *The Old Man and the Sea*, it is the unique courage of the forsaken and crucified man-God that takes his attention.... We are part of a universe offering no assurance beyond the grave, and we are to make what we can of life by a pragmatic ethic spun bravely out of man himself in full and steady cognizance that the end is darkness (299).

Courage, endurance, and acting one's part honestly and well in the face of serious obstacles and problems offer the only hope against the enveloping *nada* according to Hemingway. A good example is Golz in *For Whom the Bell Tolls*, who says, "*Bon. Nous ferons notre petite possible*" (Good, you do what little is possible), knowing well that his projected attack is doomed to failure. It is a case of courage in the face of despair. Courage is central to Hemingway's attitude to life. This is clear from his introduction to *Men at War:*

> I was very ignorant at nineteen and had read little and I remember the sudden happiness and the feeling of having a permanent protecting talisman when a young British officer I met in the hospital first wrote out for me, so that I could remember them, these lines:
>
> "By my troth, I care not; a man can die but once: we owe God a death.... and let it go which way it will, he that dies this year is quit for the next."
>
> That is probably the best thing that is written in this book and with nothing else, a man can get along all right on that (xiv).

Courage is associated with manhood, which is closely related to sex, and the Spanish term, *cojones*, which is repeatedly used in *Death in the Afternoon*, *To Have and Have Not*, and

For Whom the Bell Tolls has a relevance to both courage and sex. Sex and love figure importantly in most of Hemingway's fiction along with the gloomy theme of *nada*, night, and death. If the latter represents the dark side of Hemingway's fiction, the former, together with courage, represents the bright side—the clean well-lighted place.

The love-and-sex-theme passes through four broad forms: sex with love (Brett and Romero, Brett and Mike in *The Sun Also Rises*), sex without love (Brett and Cohn in *The Sun Also Rises*, the homosexuals and the rich in *To Have and Have Not*), love with sex (Henry and Catherine in *A Farewell to Arms*, Harry and his wife in *To Have and Have Not*, Jordan and Maria in *For Whom the Bell Tolls*, and Cantwell and Renata in *Across the River and into the Trees*), and love without sex (Brett and Jake in *The Sun Also Rises*, and Santiago in *The Old Man and the Sea*). In the short stories, the love-and-sex-theme is related to disillusionment and irony and, in the novels, it is related to a conflict between love and violence or war, which runs parallel to the theme of the clean well-lighted place amid the encircling gloom. Love is always under the threat of violence or war even as the clean well-lighted place is under constant threat from the advancing shadows of *nada*. Love is found in the gigantic, ruthless arms of war and violence. Carlos Baker, in his book, *Ernest Hemingway: The Writer as Artist* calls this "the Heloisa-Abelard relationship" and the sacrifice of Venus on the altar of Mars" (92).

This is the central motif of *A Farewell to Arms* and *For Whom the Bell Tolls*. The narrative pattern superimposed upon this theme is like the golden net, in which Hephaestus traps Aphrodite and Ares together, from which they cannot escape.

THE GROWTH OF A YOUNG BOY INTO A HERO

Hemingway shows us the growth of a young boy called Nick Adams through violence, suffering and love in his stories. It begins with his initiation into a knowledge of physical pain and death in "Indian camp", progresses through an adolescent love-affair, an interesting encounter with a crazy boxer, participation and injury in the war, prospect of fatherhood and its consequences and traumatic neurosis and the therapeutic pastime of trout-fishing to a father's reminiscences of his boyhood sexual experiences.

The story of Nick follows the same pattern as the age-old mythic hero's, analysed by Joseph Campbell as involving separation, initiation and encounter with fabulous forces, and return (30). While the mythical hero returns with extraordinary knowledge and the power to bestow boons or with a great message, the Hemingway hero returns with physical and psychic scars from his hazardous adventures. He cannot heal or help others like the mythic hero, but spends his time recuperating his physical and mental health. The injury Nick suffers in Chapter VI of *In our Time* becomes a recurring theme in Hemingway's works. All his heroes are wounded in some degree or other, at some point in their lives. They survive the wound and allow it to sink into their psyche. The wound serves as the initiation ceremony. It is generally a prelude to love as in *A Farewell to Arms*, in which the hero demonstrates true love after the wound illustrating the Priest's definition of love: "When you love, you wish to do things for. You wish to sacrifice for. You wish to serve" (60). Love follows the wound in *The Sun Also Rises*, *To Have and Have Not*, *Across the River and into the Trees* and *The Old Man and the Sea*, but in *For Whom the Bell Tolls*, the wound *seems* to follow love though, in fact, the hero shows a superior love after the wound.

When the Hemingway hero returns with his superior knowledge and love, he does not get a hero's welcome like the mythic hero. There is a sad irony about this modern hero. He grows through trials and tribulations involving physical and psychic wounds towards individuation, disillusionment, knowledge, and love. The focus is on his pilgrimage from the gloom of selfishness, dishonesty, violence, suffering, and despair to the light of courage, knowledge, and love. He is not an extraordinary man born to do great deeds, neither a Buddha nor a Napoleon, but an ordinary man of average intelligence and abilities, starting as a young boy called Nick Adams and ending up as Santiago, the old fisherman, who learns a great deal on the Gulf Stream and demonstrates an indomitable spirit. In the course of his development, he appears in different incarnations, caught up in the vortex of a world torn by violence and war—Jake trying hard to live with his incurable and unspeakable private wound, Frederic Henry trying to strike a compromise between the priest's ideal of love and Rinaldi's philosophy of life, Harry Morgan valuing courage above honesty, and Jordan and Cantwell, who act with the right mixture of courage and love. The greatest aid that the hero can find in his struggles is self-control and efficiency, cultivated as ends in themselves.

A CONTRAPUNTAL THEME

Self-control, efficiency in what one does, courage, endurance, and love—these virtues make a clean, well-lighted place which can keep off the *nada*. Hemingway is keenly conscious of the ironic juxtaposition between the lost generation and the abiding earth, and seems to say that all generations are lost against the abiding earth just as the palm-fronds of our victories, the worn light bulbs of our discoveries, and the empty condoms of our great love are lost against the Gulf Stream.

The way Hemingway employs his techniques of ironic juxtaposition, objective and dramatic correlatives, symbolistic and stylistic devices, and point of view is best appreciated only when one has a knowledge of his contrapuntal theme, which is epitomized in the Gulf Stream passage and the juxtaposition of the epigraphs introducing *The Sun Also Rises*.

This contrapuntal theme operates at two levels in Hemingway's work. At one level it is expressed by the contrast and conflict between *nada*, night, fear, despair and death, which form the gloomy side of life on the one hand, and, on the other, a self-imposed code of conduct, courage, endurance and love, heroic qualities that go into the making of a clean, well-lighted place, which can dispel the gloom. This falls into the pattern of the age-old manichean conflict between good and evil, which is the basic theme in most great literature. At another, morally and spiritually higher, level is the Ecclesiastesian theme of the antithesis between the ephemeral generations and the everlasting earth, of the futility of all human endeavour against the "one single lasting thing, the stream".

The progress from *nada* of the early fiction to agape of *The Old Man and the Sea* calls to mind the words of Milarepa, the great Bodhisattava, quoted by Joseph Campbell from *Tibet's Great Yogi Milarepa*: "If ye realize the Emptiness of all things, Compassion will arise within your hearts" (160).

5

A Farewell to Arms: The Story in Brief

The action of all Hemingway's novels is set in some foreign locale or other, and *A Farewell to Arms* is no exception. The story, here, takes place mostly in Italy and ends in Switzerland. The story is told in the first person by the protagonist.

The story opens in *medias res* during a lull in the hostilities between Italy and Austria when Italy was ruled by a weak monarch, who was controlled by the generals. In the storyteller's ironic words,

> ... if one of the officers in the back was very small and sitting between two generals, he himself so small that you could not see his face but only the top of his cap and his narrow back, and if the car went especially fast it was probably the king. He lived in Udine, and came out in this way nearly every day to see how things were going, and things went very badly (8).

Things went very badly but the king could see precious little as he was sandwiched between two generals. Then the rains came followed by cholera and "only seven thousand died of it in the army" (8).

The narrator, Frederic Henry, was an American serving as a lieutenant in the Italian Ambulance Corps. The troops took advantage of the lull in fighting, forced by the snowfall in the Alps, and passed their time in drinking and debauchery. Some of them took special pleasure in teasing the chaplain of the company, a young priest from Abruzzi. Frederic Henry respected the priest from Abruzzi, where it was clear, cold and dry and people respected you. Frederic says about him: "He had always known what I did not know and what, when I learned it, I was always able to forget. But I did not know that then, although I learned it later." Frederic went on leave but, instead of going to Abruzzi, where he was expected by the priest's father, he went to cities like Milan, Florence, Rome and Naples drowning himself in drink and debauchery, which he regretted. After his return from leave he learnt about an English nurse called Catherine Barkley, whom his doctor-friend, Rinaldi, said that he loved and wanted to marry. Rinaldi introduced Frederic to Catherine. At their first meeting, Frederick found her beautiful and contemplated a light affair with her. At their second meeting, she was cold and hostile in the beginning but, later, thawed, accepted his embrace and kiss, and expressed her love for him. Frederic still did not change his attitude that he was having a trifling affair with her: "This was a game, like bridge, in which you said things instead of playing cards" (28). He entertained fantasies of spending a night with her in bed in a hotel in Milan. But at the unconscious level he felt the stirrings of love. He felt lonely and empty when, on his next visit, Miss Ferguson told him that Catherine could not see him:

> I went out the door and suddenly I felt lonely and empty. I had treated seeing Catherine, very lightly. I had gotten somewhat drunk and nearly forgotten to come but when I could not see her there I was feeling lonely and hollow (36).

A few days later, Frederic was ordered to the front. On his way to the front he stopped his car at the British Hospital and saw her. She gave him a Saint Anthony as a protective talisman and waved him goodbye. There was a mortar attack by the Austrians at the front. Frederic and other ambulance drivers sat in a dug out eating macaroni and cheese. A mortar shell exploded nearby seriously wounding him in the legs and killing one of the drivers. He was taken to the field hospital in an ambulance. The soldier in the stretcher above him suffered a hemorrhage and his blood dripped down on Frederic. The soldier died before reaching the hospital. Before he was shifted to the general hospital in Milan, Frederic had been visited by his friends, Rinaldi and the priest. Rinaldi teased him about sex, but the priest urged him to seek a higher kind of love—love, which involves service and sacrifice—words which were to have a profound influence on Frederic.

Catherine was transferred to a hospital in Milan and came to see him. Frederic suddenly realized that he was really in love with her. The old feeling that it was a fun-game was no longer there. They made love in Frederic's hospital bed. Now he was deeply in love. "God knows that I had not wanted to fall in love with her. I had not wanted to fall in love with anyone. But God knows I had... " (75).

Next morning three doctors came and examined him. They were agreed that he should wait for six months before he could be operated on. Then a fourth doctor called Dr. Valentine came, saw his knee and operated on it next morning. During the summer, the love between Frederic and Catherine gained a great intensity. He wanted to marry her but she did not think it necessary:

> '...What good would it do to marry now? We're really married. I couldn't be any more married.'
>
> 'I only wanted to for you.'
>
> 'There is n't any me. I'm you. Don't make up a separate me' (90).

Their's was a marriage of hearts far better than a marriage in a church. Frederic was truly concerned for her but her love for him was too deep for any concerns or rituals:

> 'Couldn't we be married privately some way? Then if anything happened to me or if you had a child ...'
>
> 'There is no way to be married except by church or state. We are married privately. You see, darling, it would mean everything to me if I had any religion. But I haven't any religion.'
>
> 'Then nothing worries you?'
>
> 'Only being sent away from you. You're my religion. You're all I've got' (91).

The purity of their relationship is set off by the gross materialism symbolized by Ettore with his greed for glory and the corruption of the horse races.

Catherine became pregnant. Frederic, though disturbed by the news at first, found that he too wanted the child.

Frederic returned to duty after his convalescence. Meanwhile, the Germans broke through the Italian lines and forced a general retreat—the well-known Caporetto retreat. There were many deserters from the army. The panicky peasants joined the retreating troops in large numbers.

They came with their families and household goods, pet animals and birds trying to run away from the Austrians and the Germans.

The continuous rain, which served as a symbol of disaster all through, did not help in anyway. Two sergeants, who could not find their unit, and two girls wanted a lift on the car and got it. Frederic's truck got stuck and he ordered the two sergeants to cut brush to support the wheels. They ignored him and tried to walk away as deserters. Frederic warned them, and when they did not heed his warning, shot and wounded one of them. Bonello, his sergeant, shot the other sergeant dead.

Now the deserters' number was increasing, and the Carabinieri, the Italian Battle Police, came into the picture. They arrested the deserters and summarily executed them. At a bridge on the river, Tagliamento, Frederic was arrested by them. While awaiting interrogation, he escaped from them and jumped into the river. Braving the gun fire of the Battle Police, he swam to safety, discarded his uniform and rode to freedom under the canvas covering the guns on a gun train. Thus, like Nick in one of the sketches, he made a separate peace. "You were out of it now. You had no more obligation", he thought. This was his farewell to arms. He sought comfort and joy in the arms of his beloved. At Milan he learnt that Catherine and Helen Ferguson had gone to Stresa in the Italian lake country. When he was reunited with her at Stresa, his joy knew no bounds. In Catherine's company he was no longer lonely, but he knew that the world would not tolerate so much of happiness.

> If people bring so much courage to this world, the world has to kill them to break them, so of course it kills them. The world breaks everyone and afterward many are strong at the broken places. But those that will not break it kills (193).

Their life at Stresa was happy. He met the Count Greffi, who was ninety-four years old. They played billiards and talked about books, religion, soul, wisdom and cynicism. Count Greffi said that he had outlived his religion. Frederic said that his religion came only at night. The count said that love was a religious feeling. They became good friends in spite of the difference in age. Count Greffi's faith was not traditional but he believed firmly in life lived honestly and well.

The same evening Frederic was warned by the hotel-keeper of his imminent arrest as a deserter. A boat was provided for him and Catherine. They rowed, in the night, across Lake Maggiore, like fugitives, in the rain and the wind, to Switzerland. They were briefly detained by officers of the Swiss customs, whom they convinced that they were cousins travelling to enjoy the winter sports. They were released and took up their lodgings in a lovely chalet overlooking Montreaux. They had an idyllic time there, walking along the bank of the lake and watching the swans and gulls. January and February were idyllic months for them. When the spring rains started, Catherine's delivery time came and they left for Lausanne. Her labour pains started. They were slow and acute. As she was tired and weak, the doctor advised a Caesarian operation.

As they put a mask over her face and wheeled her stretcher into the operation room, the nurses were excited at the prospect of a Caesarian Section:

> 'It's a Caesarian', one said. 'They are going to do a Caesarian.'
>
> The other one laughed, 'We're just in time. Aren't we lucky?' (249).

As the biological trap closes on Catherine, Frederic was awfully worried. The degree of his mental tension is revealed in the following passage where he thinks in circles repeating the same fear and ineffectual autosuggestion over and over:

> Poor, poor dear Cat. And this was the price you paid for sleeping together. This was the end of the trap. This was what people got for loving each other....
>
> Yes, but what if she should die? She won't die. She's just having a bad time.... but what if she should die? She can't die.... Yes, but what if she should die? She can't, I tell you. Don't be a fool. It's just a bad time.... (246).

She was everything for him now and he could not bear the thought of her dying. This fear finds expression in the repetition of the question, 'Yes, but what if she should die?' as many as ten times in this passage.

The child was still-born and Catherine was on her death-bed. Waiting outside to hear how Catherine was, Frederic remembered how, once, he had wanted to play the Messiah for a swarm of ants struggling to escape from the fire on a log of wood by taking the log from the fire and throwing it out on the ground, but ended up throwing a tin cup of water on the log, as he wanted the cup empty for his whisky, and the water on the burning log steamed the ants to death. "Thus knowingly or unknowingly, they would kill us in the end. We would all end up like those ants", he thought. He thought, "you never had time to learn. They threw you in and told you the rules and the first time they caught you off base they killed you" (252).

He thought of God in his distress and despair and prayed to God to save Catherine: "Oh, God, please don't let her die. I'll do anything for you if you won't let her die. Please, please, Dear God, please don't let her die..." (254). He felt so emotional that words did not come to him and he repeated the same words over and over.

But there was no escape from death and Catherine knew it. She said that she was not afraid but only hated it.

She had haemorrhage after haemorrhage which the doctors could not stop. Frederic went into the room and stayed with her until she died. She was unconscious all the time and died a little later. He came out and spoke to the doctor who tried to say something about the operation. But Frederic did not want to talk about it.

When he tried to enter the room again, the nurses would not allow him. But he forced his way in and forced out the nurses. He closed the door and turned off the light, but it did not help.

"It was like saying goodbye to a statue. After a while I went out and left the hospital and walked back to the hotel in the rain" (256).

Thus ends one of the most poignant novels of love and war—love in the time of hostilities—comparable to the great classics on the same theme like *Hero and Leander*, *Troilus and Cressida*, and *Romeo and Juliet*.

6

The Dignity of the Iceberg

Anything that signifies something else is a symbol in a broad sense. A concrete thing may denote an abstraction, an event may stand for a complex situation; and a situation may have an anagogic or mystic significance. Symbolistic writing is thought-provoking and makes possible the reader's active participation in the business of literature. Symbolism is like an invisible bridge linking up the seen and the unseen, the known and the unknown. Owing to this, it may have a certain indefiniteness about it.

Edmund Wilson quotes Edgar Allan Poe's view in *Axel's Castle*: *A Study in the Imaginative Literature of 1870-1930* in this context: "I know that indefiniteness is an element of the true music [poetry]—I mean, of the true musical expression ... a suggestive indefiniteness of vague and, therefore, of spiritual effect" (13).

It involves a certain element of introspection, a certain inward searching for truths which seem to be hidden away somewhere in our psyche. This is an important strand in the American fictional tradition, the leading lights of which are Hawthorne, Poe, Melville, Mark Twain, and Henry James.

Hemingway had been taken to be a naturalistic or realistic writer for a long time until Malcolm Cowley, in his essay, "Nightmare and Ritual in Hemingway", placed him on the same shelf with Poe, Hawthorne, and Melville, "the haunted and nocturnal writers, the men who dealt in images that were symbols of an inner world" (40). Since then any number of symbolistic meanings have been read into his writings. It would be a mistake to label Hemingway as a symbolist in the sense Mallarme or Yeats or Kafka is a symbolist. In the words of Mallarme, one of symbolism's influential high priests, as quoted by Edmund Wilson,

> To name an object is to do away with the three quarters of the enjoyment of the poem which is derived from the satisfaction of guessing little by little; to suggest it, to evoke it—that is what charms the imagination (20).

Symbolism is elevated to a cult by Mallarme and the poets who came under his influence. But when stretched too far, it could cloud the meaning and lead to a total mystification of things; or the meaning in the background would overshadow the one in the foreground. Such heavy dependence on symbolistic techniques may be all right in poetry, but is, ordinarily, neither possible nor healthy in fiction, where the narrative in the foreground is of the greatest importance, for, unless it is truthfully and skilfully done, the meaning of the writer will be lost on the reader.

Hemingway is a conscious craftsman, who uses his techniques, including symbolism, in a closely controlled way even as he would handle with the greatest control a gun or a fishing rod or a glass of liquor. He is also aware of the symbols carrying more meanings than intended. He is reported to have said in a *Time* interview after winning the Nobel Prize:

> No good book has been written that has in it symbols arrived at beforehand and stuck in .... That kind of symbol sticks out like raisins in raisin bread.... I tried to make a real old man, a real boy, a real sea and a real fish and real sharks. But if I make them good and true enough, they would mean many things. The hardest thing is to make something really true, sometimes truer than true (72).

Hemingway seems to believe that what a writer makes truthfully may mean many things; he may not insert symbols intentionally in his work, but, as his conscious mind is engaged in making real things, his unconscious may sort out things in such a way that the things so made have a symbolic or ironic significance.

The writer's intellectual and moral equipment, including his training, tradition, imagination, and honesty, goes into this creative activity.

It is difficult to agree with Hemingway when he says that in a good book symbols are never arrived at beforehand and stuck in. If it were so, rain as a disaster symbol would not have been used so importantly in *A Farewell to Arms*, nor mountains as symbols of good, clean and healthy living and plains as symbols of corruption, unclean living and killing fields. If he said what he really practised, he would not have prefaced "*The Snows of Kilimanjaro*" with an epigraph containing a reference to the leopard, which has nothing to do with the story if it is not viewed as a symbol.

His theory of the iceberg throws considerable light on his techniques of understatement and symbolism. He says in *Death in the Afternoon*: "The dignity of movement of an iceberg is due to only one-eighth of it being above water" (183).

Symbolism is a suggestive device. Here the writer omits certain things and leaves it to the symbol to suggest them. It is an extreme form of understatement. A writer may have an allusion, literary or mythological or religious, in mind, or may be strongly aware of a situation, physical or psychological, but may not say it in so many words preferring instead to suggest it in a subtle way. It is like turning on a switch to make an electric bulb light up or using a remote control device to make a T.V. screen come alive.

Symbolism in fiction, together with other narrative techniques, should contribute to the meaning of the work, and the total functioning of the different narrative devices is of the nature of orchestration, producing the harmony of form in fiction generating aesthetic pleasure.

ROMANCE, MYTH AND RITUAL

Gertrude Stein says of Hemingway, in the Autobiography of Alice B. Toklas: "And that is Hemingway, he looks like a modern and he smells of museums" (216). This remark hints at certain aspects of Hemingway's work containing echoes of legend, myth and classical literature.

A course in classical literature in Sylvia Beach's bookshop and his close association with influential writers like Ezra Pound, T.S. Eliot, James Joyce, and Gertrude Stein might have stimulated his interest in mythology, legend, classics, and allusive writing. Besides, romance, myth and ritual are part of the American fictional tradition inherited by Hemingway. He lived close to the Ojibway Indians in his boyhood and the impact of their way of life on his mind might also have contributed to this interest.

Nick Adams of *In our Time* is the first Hemingway hero. In the first story of the collection, "Indian Camp", he is a young boy initiated by his own father into the mysteries of pain, birth and death, and a symbolic return to civilization equipped with a lot of unusual knowledge. His father acts as his guide and he has complete faith in his father: "In the early morning on the lake, sitting in the stern of the boat with his father rowing, he felt quite sure that he would never die (21). Later on, he ventures out, as a young adult and an adult, meets with more exciting experiences, including an eerie adventure with a crazy boxer, war, and traumatic neurosis following an injury in war. He recuperates on the bank of the "Big Two-Hearted River", trout-fishing, marries, and becomes a father. He returns as a preceptor and guide to his son in "Fathers and Sons", having gone out as a novice at first under the guidance of his father. The pattern of his life fits in with that of the mythical hero, as explained by Joseph Campbell, with the necessary modifications under modern conditions:

> A hero ventures forth from the world of common day into a region of supernatural wonder: fabulous forces are there encountered and a decisive victory is won: the hero comes back from this mysterious adventure with the power to bestow boons on his fellow man (30).

Nick goes into the wide world, like a Jason or a Theseus, obeying the call of adventure, faces the horrors of pain and death or an ogre of a battler or a psychic monster like traumatic neurosis or *nada*, and returns. This mythical journey recurs again and again in all of Hemingway's novels. But the modern hero's adventure is only with the strange and the fearful; his victory is only survival; and his knowledge is only disillusionment. There is the mythical contact with water forming part of the initiation into a new life in almost all his works. In "Indian Camp", *A Farewell to Arms*, *To Have and Have Not*, *Across the River and into the Trees*, and *The Old Man and the Sea*, water figures prominently, virtually enveloping action, while in *The Sun Also Rises* and *For Whom the Bell Tolls*, it is limited to a symbolic contact signifying initiation. Water figures importantly in mythical and religious rites as an instrument of initiation. Contact with it is a kind of baptismal or purificatory rite preparing the hero for an adventure or marking an important change in his worldview or personality.

In *A Farewell to Arms*, the hero's plunge into the Tagliamento marks a turning point in his life. The river takes him to another, new, life. Later, the hero and the heroine travel on the lake in rough weather from Italy to Switzerland. Apart from their transport to another country and another life, it marks the beginning of another adventure. All the while the rain which signifies disaster acts as an enveloping symbol.

"Big Two-Hearted River" is a story in which everything, from camping to fishing, is elevated to an elaborate ritual. It symbolizes a return to nature and its therapeutic benefits and a desire on the part of the protagonist to live in harmony with nature. The primitive people believed that elaborate ceremonies and rituals helped them in learning to live in harmony with nature.

It was a way of acknowledging the supremacy of the abiding earth and paying homage to it. The initiation rites make the whole society visible to itself as an imperishable living unit. Joseph Campbell has this to say on the initiation rites and seasonal rites:

> Generations of individuals pass, like anonymous cells from a living body but the sustaining, timeless form remains.... It has been customary to describe the seasonal

> festivals of so-called native peoples as efforts to control nature. This is a misrepresentation.... the dominant motive in all truly religious (as opposed to black-magical) ceremonial is that of submission to the inevitables of destiny—and in the seasonal festivals this motive is particularly apparent (383-384).

As Nick carefully takes hold of the hopper by the wings in "Big Two-Hearted River", or as Jake digs for worms on the grassy bank of the stream at Burguete, or as Frederic takes off his wet coat, trousers, wallet, papers, money, shirt and underclothing and puts them on again, cutting the cloth-stars off carefully, or as Jordan holds on to himself very carefully and delicately to keep his hands steady, or as Cantwell shuts the car door carefully and well before his death, it is of this ritual that we are reminded—the ritual of doing things with a deliberation, imparting an aura of significance to common actions. This ritualized activity is the formula for the emotion the primitive man felt at the time of the initiation rites and the seasonal rituals. It is the apotheosis of the continual form of the community or the flux of life and of the abiding earth as opposed to the passing generations of individuals. Man who is marked for death from the moment of his birth has to make a compromise and live in harmony with those inevitables of destiny until he becomes part of the everlasting earth.

Jake of *The Sun Also Rises* is the Fisher-King of the Grail Legend, whose wound and impotence symbolize the sterility of a generation. T.S. Eliot uses this motif, as well as others, in his *The Waste Land*. In such references to myth, ritual and legend, Hemingway's technique is very close to Eliot's use of the objective correlative for the emotion involved. But Hemingway is a more rigid symbolist than Eliot since he not only does not provide the reader with any clue to the meaning but makes it very difficult for him to detect the symbols, which are generally hidden away under a surface story—a truthful rendition of what actually happens and what really produces the emotion which is felt. The symbols are there at the bottom like the trout which Nick does not see at first in "Big Two-Hearted River" of *In our Time*:

> At the bottom of the pool were the big trout. Nick did not see them at first. Then he saw them at the bottom of the pool, big trout looking to hold themselves on the gravel bottom in a varying mist of gravel and sand, raised in spurts by the current (178).

Nick is like a student of literature looking for hidden meanings in a work of art. He watches the trout "keeping themselves steady in the current with wavering fins", and then he sees many trout in deep, fast moving water, but does not suspect the presence of the big trout at the bottom. Then they appear "in a varying mist of gravel and sand" like symbolic meanings hiding under a lucid style. Nick progresses to this discovery from the easily observable trout in the current, which are like symbolic referents in literature.

The following passage in *A Farewell to Arms* is a good example of how Hemingway celebrates the seasons—autumn changing into winter—by presenting an oak forest destroyed by the war at the end of the fall when the snow comes down like a shroud to cover the dead forest, and the dying year. He does not say it in so many words, but makes the forest and the snow act it out by describing in bare, bald language how it happened:

> The forest of oak trees on the mountain beyond the town was gone. The forest had been green in the summer when we had come into the town but now there were the stumps and the broken trunks and the ground torn up, and one day at the end of the fall when I was out where the oak forest had been I saw a cloud coming over the mountain. It came very fast and the sun went a dull yellow and then everything was grey and the sky was covered and the cloud came on down the mountain and suddenly we were in it and it was snow (9).

Where there was a forest there are only stumps and broken trunks and torn up ground. The forest is gone. It is the end of the fall. The fall of the forest as well as the commencement of winter with snowfall is indicated by the word "fall" used skilfully between the description of the ruined forest and that of the descending snow. The remains of the forest are to be covered by a winding sheet and down comes the snow. The coming of the snow is described as it is seen and felt by the narrator. We are there with Frederic Henry in what had been an oak forest and then we see through his consciousness a cloud over the mountain at first. Then the cloud comes very fast towards us, and the sun turns a dull yellow. We, in Henry's consciousness, look around. Everything is grey; the sky is covered; the cloud comes down and envelops us and then we know it is the snow.

There are only visual impressions here. The writer describes what actually happened in the place where there had been an oak forest. But when the snow comes, first as a white cloud, and a little while later, covering everything, we find that it symbolizes a shroud signifying the death of the forest, and of the year. The seasons are subtly suggested. The oak forest 'falls' in the fall. The fall which signifies the fall of leaves here signifies the fall of the forest itself at the end of which ("at the end of the fall") the snow comes and acts as a shroud.

We have to read between the lines to discover the symbols and the suggested meanings. The writer does not help us by giving any clues.

In *The Sun Also Rises*, Jake's fishing at Burguete, like Nick's in "Big Two-Hearted River" is a ritual in homage to nature. Jake reveals himself as a Fisher-King with a difference. His wound is incurable, and he learns to live with it in harmony with the abiding earth and the flux of life around him. The references to myth and ritual are at the secondary level, along with objective and dramatic correlatives, like the many trout which Nick sees in deep, fast moving water. At the tertiary level are the psychological, religious, or anagogic symbols like the big trout at the bottom. The story which is a truthful rendition of actions, sensations, and emotions is at the primary level.

The references to myth and ritual provide a broad objective correlative for Hemingway's contrapuntal theme by making the reader recapture, or at least feel vaguely stirring within him, the pristine emotions related to the community ceremonies like the initiation and the seasonal rites.

RELIGIOUS SYMBOLISM

Hemingway's fiction up to *For Whom the Bell Tolls* smacks of *The Old Testament* symbolism, myth and ritual having more importance than in the last two novels, which have a Christological symbolism. This tendency reveals itself in *For Whom the Bell Tolls*, which acts as a bridge between the first three major works (four, if *In our Time* is included) and the last two. It is interesting to note that the bridge is the central symbol in *For Whom the Bell Tolls*. Nick Adams is the hero of many Hemingway stories. His surname suggests *The Old Testament* name of Adam, the first man or the generic man. Hemingway's biblical narrative starts with Adam's initiation to a knowledge of birth and death, and, later, his fall from the freight train when he is thrown out by the brakeman. Adam becomes Jacob (Jake) in *The Sun Also Rises*. As Jacob wrestles with God "until the breaking of the day" (Genesis, 32: 24-30), Jake wrestles with his own consciousness all the night. The blessing he receives in the end is disillusionment, another name for the knowledge and understanding that pain is the condition of life and has to be endured without complaint.

Once the general suggestiveness of Hemingway's titles and proper nouns is accepted, a continuity of religious symbolism can be seen in Hemingway's novels. Jake Barnes of *The Sun Also Rises* is Jacob with a difference—a barren Jacob in the manner of T.S. Eliot's impotent Fisher-King. He becomes Frederic Henry in *A Farewell to Arms* who is baptized in rain and the river, Tagliamento, and walks back to his hotel in the rain, chastened by the pain of bereavement. He becomes Harry Morgan who has his baptism in the Gulf Stream and realizes, before his death, that wrong-doing and working alone do not lead one anywhere. That leads us to Robert Jordan, the hero of *For Whom the Bell Tolls* whose name suggests the holy river that baptized Jesus Christ. *For Whom the Bell Tolls* carries a passage from Donne, as its epigraph, which emphasizes the oneness of all mankind and the Christian ideal of sacrifice. Jordan stands between Jake and Santiago like the baptizing river which separates and joins Israel (Jacob) and the apostle, St. James (Santiago), as well as *The Old Testament* and *The New Testament*.

The kind of love expounded by the priest in *A Farewell to Arms* ["When you love you wish to do things for. You wish to sacrifice for. You wish to serve" (60)] begins to bloom in *For Whom the Bell Tolls*. Mythological symbols yield place to religious and Christological symbols. The rain in *A Farewell to Arms*, which is generally interpreted as a symbol of disaster and death, is a symbol of baptism and rebirth also. This novel-length baptism finds its personification in Robert Jordan, who represents its flowering by his sense of love which rises above lust and passion and by his martyrdom. Rain does not figure in the last three novels. Its purpose having been served as an instrument of baptism, rain is no longer needed, and the Christological figure peeps out occasionally through Robert Jordan, Col. Cantwell, and Santiago.

Mary is a recurring religious symbol in *For Whom the Bell Tolls*. The heroine's name, Maria, suggests the Virgin. Her violation is a sacrilege and symbolizes the curse on Spain. The cruelties and humiliations she suffers prior to the outrage put us in mind of the ill-treatment meted out to Jesus before the crucifixion. Her recuperation in three days through the Christian virtue of love is a parallel to the resurrection. People in distress pray to Virgin Mary. In *Across the River and into the Trees*, Col. Cantwell's last three days are packed with love and forgiveness. He makes a conscious effort not to be bitter about things. His bad hand, which Renata loves much and which he uses to satisfy her while foregoing his own sexual fulfilment, is like the nailed hand of Jesus.

In *The Old Man and the Sea*, Santiago (Saint James) is called "the best fisherman", a sobriquet given to Jesus, who taught fishermen like Peter, Andrew, John and James, how to catch men and become the fishermen of men. The Christian symbolism shifts back and forth between the marlin and Santiago. The marlin is nailed (harpooned) first. Santiago settles against the wood of the bow and takes his suffering as it comes like Jesus on the cross. Santiago's wounded hands, his climbing up the road with the mast on his shoulder, his falling under its weight, and the way he lies in his shack "with his arms out straight and the palms of his hands up", all remind us of the crucifixion episode. The biblical numerology in Santiago fishing with the boy for *forty* days, and fishing alone for *forty-four* days, struggling with the marlin for *three* days, and landing him on the *seventh* attempt, killing *seven* sharks, and resting *seven* times, is interesting, as pointed out by Joseph Waldmeir (162).

The three-day span of action in the last three novels points to the Christological entombment symbol.

PSYCHO-ANALYTICAL SYMBOLISM

There have been many attempts to read Freudian and Jungian meanings into Hemingway's fiction. The psycho-analytical method throws light on certain situations and reveals new meanings though it could be, sometimes, stretched too far. Psychological symbolism in a work of art is more the critic's concern than the writer's, for it involves the writer's unconscious as well as the character's, and the writer is generally not conscious of it when he uses it. Conscious or unconscious, he is caught in his own trap, for the critic probes the writer's unconscious as well.

In *The Sun Also Rises*, the predicament of Jake and Brett, which is central to the novel, is effectively demonstrated by the striking parallel between the human situation and the *Corrida de Toros*. Jake likens a bull to a boxer like Cohn. He himself is like a steer. The division of the novel into three books parallels the three divisions of a bullfight; Cohn, Mike, and Romero are like the three bulls a bullfighter gets in one afternoon. Brett is the *vaquilla* or the female of the fighting bull and Jake the *cabestro* or the trained steer. Robert Lewis, Jr. (32-33) and Dewey Ganzel (26-48) discuss this symbolism in detail. Dewey Ganzel stresses caution and control as central to the role of a *cabestro* and says that Jake plays that role very well with "grace under pressure" (28).

The newly leaved chestnuts around the statue of Marshal Ney are interpreted as a phallic emblem by R.W. Stallman (183). Marshal Ney's gesture with the sword and the raised baton of the mounted policeman at the end of the novel are also phallic symbols. The mounted policeman's raised baton is described as a "wonderfully suggestive gesture, both phallic and symbolic of the new command that Jake has issued to himself", by Earl Rovit (158), as the "ironic phallic symbol" by John S. Rouch (368), and as the phallic baton "by Robert W. Lewis, Jr. (213). Dewey Ganzel is of the view that it is a symbol of external control and recollected responsibility (46). Mark Spilka thinks that the mounted policeman stands for war and the society which made it (91). P.G. Rama Rao points out that it is an effective dramatic correlative for the situation of the leading characters and for what happens at the moment in their consciousness, and that the policeman with his baton is a symbol which lights up the entire novel and gives it a new dimension stressing the importance of direction and control if life is to have any meaning in a world where all is vanity (69).

The phallic symbol becomes part of the Hemingway hero's personal equipment as Frederic Henry's pistol, Harry Morgan's gun, Robert Jordan's dynamite packs and machine gun, Col. Cantwell's gun and Santiago's harpoon.

In the first chapter of *A Farewell to Arms*, the marching soldiers, looking like pregnant ladies, with cartridge boxes bulging under their capes, serve as a dramatic correlative for the story of Frederic Henry and Catherine—the man with the pistol and the cartridge that causes conception and death. Later, when Henry is on the point of leaving Catherine, now three months gone with child, for the front, he buys a pistol and cartridges, and the purchase, made in the company of Catherine, occupies nearly two pages (116-17). This episode underlines the importance of the cartridges with their already established association with pregnancy as an objective correlative for the condition of Catherine, who carries in her womb the cartridge that will eventually kill her. Thus, the symbol of union and generation stands for separation and death also. Creation bears within itself the seeds of destruction.

In *For Whom the Bell Tolls*, destruction leads to another kind of creation, and separation to a different kind of union. Robert Jordan's use of his dynamite, grenades and machine gun are counterbalanced by his assurances to Maria that he is in her, and the phallic symbol, which destroys and kills, now covers her escape from death. She is asked to believe that she carries both Jordan and herself in her: "As long as there is one of us there is both of us" (463).

In *The Old Man and the Sea*, when Santiago's phallic harpoon penetrates the marlin so deep that he feels the marlin's heart, he not only kills but achieves a union beyond sex. It makes him feel a brotherly love and a sense of identification with the fish. What kills also creates at a higher level.

The sleeping bag in *For Whom the Bell Tolls*, the blanket in the gondola in *Across the River and into the Trees,* and the sea in *The Old Man and the Sea* are interpreted as womb symbols indicating a desire for regression or reversion to the intra-uterine state. John Killinger regards the sleeping bag a womb symbol and calls the sea "a primordial womb symbol" (27, 48). Earl Rovit is of the same view and equates Renata with the mother-image and Cantwell's alter-ego or *anima*, and concludes that, in *The Old Man and the Sea,* the regression of the tyro figure is complete with the heroine assuming her primordial symbolic form as *la mar*, the eternal, feminine sea (66). Rovit goes further and sees patricide and matricide in the symbolic construct of *A Farewell to Arms*; he calls the sergeant, whom Henry shoots and the battle police father-images refers to it as the tyro's revolt against the tutor, symbolically killing one of his manifestations, and says that the tyro indirectly destroys his mother and *anima* in the novel (69). Stanley Cooperman describes Henry's injury as technological rape, his recuperation and love as restoration of his manhood through Catherine, and Catherine's death as Henry's final, spiritual castration (182-84). Henry and Catherine being inside her hair which forms a kind of tent over them, while they make love, may be taken as a womb symbol:

> I loved to take her hair down and she sat on the bed and kept very still except suddenly she would dip down to kiss me while I was doing it, and I would take out the pins and lay them on the sheet and it would be loose and I would watch her while she kept very still and then take out the last two pins and it would all come down and she would drop her head and we would both be inside of it, and it was the feeling of inside a tent or behind a falls (89).

Psycho-analytical criticism is a slippery playground and, while such interpretations are quite possible and could be reasonable to some extent, there is always the danger of the critic or the reader playing the role of a psychiatrist treating the writer as a patient turning this variety of criticism into a psychiatrist's couch.

OTHER FORMS OF SYMBOLISM: OBJECTIVE AND DRAMATIC CORRELATIVES

Some of Hemingway's titles and the names of some characters have a symbolic or ironic significance. As a conscious craftsman he seems to have taken some pains to give meaningful names to some of his characters with a special intent. Thus, Jake Barnes is a barren Jacob representing the wasteland of a war-ravaged generation; Pilar is the Blessed Virgin of Pilar, the mother-figure for the Christ-surrogates, Maria and Jordan, and the guerillas. Jordan is the river that baptized Jesus and links the Jews and the Muslims, and Robert Jordan is the link between the guerillas and the outside world, and also between Jacob and Santiago; Richard Cantwell, once referred to as Richard, the Lion-Hearted, suffers from a bad heart and cannot get well; Renata or "the reborn", a sort of presiding genius of Venice, is Venice Reborn, as her portrait suggests, and also Cantwell's youth reborn; Jackson, by nominal association with Stonewall Jackson, signifies the death of a perfect soldier; Manolin, the alter-ego of Santiago, is Manolo or Manuel Garcia, the undefeated bullfighter; and Santiago is a lesser Saint James.

A T.S. Eliot type of allusiveness, achieved through playing with quotations, can be seen in some of Hemingway's titles. *In our Time*, taken from *The Book of Common Prayer* ("Give peace in our Time, O Lord") is an ironic echo of the prayer, calling our attention to the absence of peace in our time. The title of the story, "In Another Country" is derived from Marlowe's *The Jew of Malta*:

> Friar Barnardine: Thou hast committed—
> Barabas: Fornication? But that was in another country: and besides the wench is dead (Act I, sc. I, ll. 39-41)

This quotation finds its echo in Bill's playful remark in *The Sun Also Rises*: "That was in another country. And besides all the animals were dead (77). The story of *A Farewell to Arms* reads like an expansion of the quotation from *The Jew of Malta*. Catherine of Scotland and Henry of the U.S.A. fall in love with each other in another country, Italy. They are not married and when they make love, it is fornication. The wench, Catherine, dies in the end.

"Cat in the Rain" from *In our Time* is a story which illustrates Hemingway's symbolistic technique. It is about an American couple who are stopping over at a hotel. Their room is on the second floor facing the sea and the public garden and war monument. The garden and the monument are symbols of artificial comfort while the sea is the sea of despair. They are childless, and the wife asks for a kitty. The cat is a substitute for a baby. The American wife has to choose between despair and artificial comfort. Her natural feminine cravings like having a baby, growing out her hair, and having a home of her own are stifled and she is told to be content with reading (a substitute for living) and a tortoise-shell cat (a substitute for a cat which is a substitute for a child) presented to her by the padrone (a God-Surrogate).

The empty square is a dramatic correlative for the emptiness of her life. The rain which keeps on pouring throughout the story symbolizes the wretchedness of the American wife.

There appears some association in Hemingway's mind between "Cat in the rain" and Catherine of *A Farewell to Arms* (called Cat by Henry). Catherine sometimes sees herself and Henry dead in the rain. Hemingway uses rain as an important symbol for the first time in "Cat in the Rain" and, later, as a major symbol in *A Farewell to Arms*.

Another major symbol in *A Farewell to Arms* is that of the mountain as contrasted with the plain. Carlos Baker discusses this symbol elaborately in *Hemingway: The Writer as Artist*. He relates the mountain vs. plain symbolism to the opposed concepts of Home and Not-Home:

> The Home-Concept, for example, is associated with the mountains; with dry-cold weather; with peace and quiet; with love, dignity, health, happiness, and the good life; and with worship or at least the consciousness of God. The Not-Home concept is associated with low-lying plains; with rain and fog; with obscenity, indignity, disease, suffering, nervousness, war and death; and with irreligion (102).

The mountains are associated with decent, good, and happy life. The priest, the code hero who teaches the meaning of love to Henry, comes from the mountain country of Abruzzi. When Henry goes on leave, the priest advises him to go to Abruzzi and even writes to his father. But Henry does not go to Abruzzi even though he wants to go there. He does not go to Abruzzi, where the roads are frozen and it is clear, cold and dry and where one is respected. Instead he goes to the cities, to the smoke of cafés and lecherous nights in the plains.

Henry and Catherine live an idyllic life in a brown wooden house in the pine trees on the side of the mountain in Switzerland. The prospect is beautiful. They eat their breakfast looking at the lake and the mountains across the lake on the French side (222). But when the labour pains start, they go down to the hospital in the city of Lousanne where tragedy strikes.

The mountain vs. plain symbol is an integral symbol, which has an important bearing on the meanings of not only

A Farewell to Arms but *The Sun Also Rises*, and *For Whom the Bell Tolls*. In *The Old Man and the Sea* also there is a symbolic ascent made by Santiago to his shack. The mountain, by its very elevation, symbolizes the apotheosis of the abiding earth, which serves as a backdrop for the human drama presented by Hemingway.

When asked about the symbolism in his writing, Hemingway tells George Plimpton: "I suppose there are symbols since critics keep finding them .... Read anything I write for the pleasure of reading it. Whatever else you find will be the measure of what you brought to the reading" (29).

7

A Style-Making Mastery of the Art of Modern Narration

When Hemingway won the Nobel Award in 1954, the citation included a reference to his "powerful style-making mastery of the art of modern narration." His unique style was noticed even during his Paris days when his first important work, *In our Time* was published. Archibald Macleish's tribute to his style was reported in *Time*:

> Veteran out of the wars before he was twenty:
> Famous at twenty-five: thirty a master—
> Whittled a style for his time from a walnut stick
> In a carpenter's loft in a street of the April city.

Hemingway's ambition was to achieve new dimensions in prose-writing—a fourth and a fifth dimension if possible. In his *Green Hills of Africa* the first-person narrator says: "The kind of writing that can be done. How far prose can be carried if anyone is serious enough and has luck. There is a fourth and fifth dimension that can be gotten" (26-27).

Hemingway's contrapuntal theme of the human drama against the backdrop of the everlasting earth or the sea or the flux of life, the horological time versus the geological time seems to determine his style which also has a dialectic about it—a two-faced style. One face of it is evocative, hard boiled and masculine. The everlasting background demands a tight-lipped, well-honed, masculine prose while the human drama requires an evocative, romantic, feminine prose. This unique style is best suited to Hemingway's theme of Aphrodite (the goddess of beauty and love) locked inescapably in the arms of Ares (the god of war)—the tender, evocative style wrapped in the embrace of the rugged simplicity of the staccato sentences. It also matches the incongruous personality of Hemingway himself, beautifully captured by the *New Yorker* cartoon, which shows a brawny forearm and hand clutching a rose, entitled "The Soul of Ernest Hemingway", to which Robert Penn Warren refers in his introduction to *A Farewell to Arms* (Scribner's, 1957 ed., xxi). Charles R. Anderson discusses the two styles of Hemingway in his famous essay, "Hemingway's Other Style", included in *Critiques of Four Major Novels* edited by Carlos Baker (New York, 1962, 41-46).

THE CULT OF SIMPLICITY

The cult of simplicity is as old as the authorized version of the *Bible*. John Bunyan and Jonathan Swift practised simplicity and made a minimum use of simile or metaphor, as figures of speech could interfere with the directness and flow of the narrative. Hemingway belongs to this stylistic tradition of simplicity. But he adheres to simplicity and concreteness more rigidly than Bunyan or Swift. His preference for concrete words, unburdened by ornamental qualifiers, intensifiers, and figures of speech can be seen in the following passage from *A Farewell to Arms*:

> The nurse opened the door and motioned with her finger for me to come. I followed her into the room. Catherine did not look up when I came in. I went over to the side of the bed. The doctor was standing by the bed on the opposite side. Catherine looked at me and smiled. I bent down over the bed and started to cry (254).

Here is no effort to introduce emotion, but only a bare action-picture of what happened—the picture which is the formula of the emotion one feels. The simplest possible words are used and the active verb is the simple past—"opened", "motioned", "followed", "came", "went", "looked", "smiled", "bent", and "started." The passage being an action-picture, the important word is the verb. The basic word is the simple verb and the basic sentence is the declarative simple sentence. Out of a total of seven sentences, there is only one complex sentence which has only one unimportant looking subordinate clause. There are two pure simple sentences and the rest are compound sentences each containing two simple sentences joined by 'and'. The technique of "Polysyndeton" with "and" as the most frequently used conjunction, is a favourite technique with Hemingway, borrowed from *The Old Testament Narratives* of his Oak Park school syllabus. This technique survives some of his stylistic changes into *The Old Man and the Sea,* and makes the verbal action-picture move fast, simple sentence after simple sentence running in quick succession, the copula, "and", audibly as well as visibly holding the different units of the picture together.

Look at the following passage in which Henry fantasizes spending a night with Catherine in a hotel room in Milan and it will be clear how wonderfully "and" works:

> ... and we would go in the front door and the porter would take off his cap and I would stop at the concierge's desk and ask for the key and she would stand by the elevator and then we would get in the elevator and it would go up very slowly clicking at all the floors and then our floor and the boy would open the door and stand there and she would step out and I would step out and we would walk down the hall ... (33).

The absence of punctuation and the coordinate "and" help in leading the reader from one picture to another without any pause until the whole picture hangs as one unit before his eyes. The copula is the non-interfering commentator's voice, now reduced to the minimum. The pictures are simply presented one by one without any commentary on their relative importance and without subordinating one image to another. "And" helps in this kind of presentation which frequently is of the nature of cinematography. Joseph Warren Beach terms this "the great levelling democracy of the *and*" (101).

Hemingway felt that words needed to be recharged as they lost their power from careless use. He says in *Death in the Afternoon* that all our words from loose using have lost their edge (72). Harry Levin calls this distrust of words "verbal skepticism" (592). Henry expresses a dislike of certain words in *A Farewell to Arms*:

> I was always embarrassed by the words sacred, glorious, and sacrifice and the expression in vain.... Abstract words such as glory, honour, courage, or hallow were obscene beside the concrete names of villages, the numbers of roads, the names of rivers, the numbers of regiments and the dates (143-144).

As an artist, Hemingway is opposed to maudlin sentiment and unrealistic romantic feelings which lead to hollow words like glory and honour. The artistry he displays in using words and the emotions he evokes by using a word, or by not using a word sometimes, reveal his faith in the magic power of the word. In "Fathers and Sons", young Nick, who is told that mashing is a heinous sin, pictures to himself Caruso, who is arrested for mashing, doing something strange with a potato masher to a beautiful lady, and resolves to try mashing at least once when he is old enough. Harry Levin observes, in this context, as follows:

> The powers of connotation, the possibilities of oblique suggestion and semantic association, are actually grasped by Hemingway as well as any writer of our time. Thus he can retrospectively endow a cheap and faded term like "mashing" with all the promise and poetry of awakening manhood (594).

In "The Sea Change", the word 'lesbian', in "Hills like Elephants", the word 'abortion', in "A Simple Inquiry", the word 'homosexual', and in "Big Two-Hearted River", the word 'war', which are vital and central to the story, are not used, but by not using these words, Hemingway makes us feel their effect all the more. This is in accordance with his iceberg theory.

THE TECHNIQUE OF REPETITION

Hemingway uses "repetition" as a stylistic device to the maximum advantage. The popular view that he imbibed it from Gertrude Stein and James Joyce is disproved by his juvenilia of the Oak Park High School days where he wrote the story "Sepi Jingan" (*Tabula,* November 16, 1916):

> Yes. He was a bad Indian. Up on the upper peninsula he couldn't get drunk. He used to drink all day—everything. But he couldn't get drunk. Then he would go crazy; but he wasn't drunk. He was crazy because he couldn't get drunk (Fenton, 26).

His use of repetition could be traced back to his freshman text of *The Old Testament Narratives.* He captures the incantatory effect of repetition so common in *The Old Testament.* It transforms language into a kind of verbal ritual with its emphasis on form—doing things carefully and correctly. Ritual is the medium of formal homage or worship or glorification. The everlasting earth or the limitless Gulf Stream representing nature and the flux of life, against which man cannot prevail, draw homage from Hemingway and the ritualistic style is the form this homage seems to take:

> And what if she should die? She won't die. People don't die in childbirth nowadays. That was what all husbands thought. Yes, but what if she should die? She won't die. She's just having a bad time. The initial labour is usually protracted. She's only having a bad time. Afterward we'd say what a bad time, and Catherine would say it wasn't really so bad. But what if she should die? She can't die. Yes, but what if she should die? She can't, I tell you. Don't be a fool. It's just a bad time. It's just nature giving her hell. It's only the first labour, which is almost always protracted. Yes, but what if she should die? She can't die. Why would she die? What reason is there for her to die? There's just a child that has to be born, the by-product of good nights in Milan (246).

The repetition in the above passage serves two purposes. It expresses a tense state of mind. The narrator's anxiety is powerfully expressed through repetition—the same question and a futile autosuggestion recurring again and again. Secondly, the ineffectuality, futility and helplessness of the characters against the background of an all-powerful nature which is responsible for Catherine's suffering. Here, nature acts as a biological trap for Catherine luring her and Henry through good nights resulting in Catherine's conception as a fatal by-product. Henry and Catherine are both helpless before this mighty cosmic force. Henry's soliloquy expresses helplessness through a repetitive style.

VERBAL ECONOMY

Hemingway's economy of expression enables him to keep out all feelings and thoughts which may come in the way of the true emotion a given situation generates. To this end, he whittles down his language to the barest minimum until it takes the form of significant understatement. His training as a reporter must have stood him in good stead in this respect. He tells us in "Old Newsman Writes: A Letter from Cuba", which appeared in *Esquire* (December 1934), how he sent a cable, "Kemal inswards unburned Smyrna Guilty Greeks", which, copyrighted by Monumental News Service, appeared in print as follows:

> Mustapha Kemal in an exclusive interview today with the correspondent of the Monumental News Service denied vehemently that the Turkish forces had any part in the burning of Smyrna. The city, Kemal stated, was fired by incendiaries in the troops of the Greek rearguard before the first Turkish Patrols entered the city (*By Line: Ernest Hemingway*, 155).

This kind of verbal compression approximates poetic expression and makes demands on the reader. In narrative prose, it results in bare depiction of action and situation free from the writer's sentiments, emotions, and comments. It helps in the dramatization of the narrative reducing summary to the barest minimum. Reader-participation is necessary here, for this method demonstrates, in a way, the classical concept of showing only the "elbows of action" to intensify the effect.

The last paragraph of the opening chapter and the last paragraph of the concluding chapter of *A Farewell to Arms* are good examples for this kind of prose:

> At the start of the winter came the permanent rain, and with the rain came the cholera. But it was checked and in the end only seven thousand died of it in the army (8).

By the time we come to the end of the opening chapter the tone is set for the novel—the commencement of winter and the never-ending rain and the cholera which had killed seven thousand men in the army, not to speak of the others, before it was checked and on top of everything the ironic tone in 'permanent rain' and 'only seven thousand.' The sentences are simple sentences held together by 'and'. Rain as a symbol of disaster is also established in the first chapter.

The last paragraph of the concluding chapter which concludes the novel itself reads thus:

> But after I had got them out and shut the door and turned off the light it wasn't any good. It was like saying good-bye to a statue. After a while I went out and left the hospital and walked back to the hotel in the rain.

The sentences in the above passage are also mostly declarative simple sentences. One is a complex sentence but a simple complex sentence with only one subordinate clause. The vocabulary, like in the passage from the opening chapter, is very simple. But the passage tells us many things. The closure of the story is signified by the shutting of the door as well as the end of a life. That the light of Catherine's life is out is signified by the narrator turning off the light. Catherine who was once alive and full of life is now like a lifeless statue. The narrator bids goodbye to her and to the readers also. His walking back alone in the rain brings us back to the killer rain of the first chapter. The narrative brings us from the 'we' of the opening sentences to the 'I' of the closing sentence indicating thereby the loss suffered by the narrator/hero. The rain does not kill him but does something worse. It marks the death of one who is more important to him than the whole world. The simple words, 'shut the door' and 'turn off the light' and 'good-bye' work like magic.

IMPRESSIONISTIC METHOD

Hemingway follows the same bare, controlled method, which in its precision takes on an impressionistic hue, piling impression on impression to make the picture. The opening paragraph of "A Way You'll Never Be" is a good example with its inventory of impressions. In "Big Two-Hearted River", Nick, who returns to Seney finds no town but the burned over country as he sits, a pathetic figure, on his bundle of canvas and bedding. He sees no trace of the thirteen saloons that had lined the one street of Seney but only the foundations of the Mansion House with the stone chipped and split by the fire. Later sooty, black grasshoppers are added to the list of these impressions.

In *A Farewell to Arms*, there is a bare, bald description of an oak forest destroyed by the war, and we find Hemingway doing remarkable things under the surface of this description. Even though this passage was quoted in the chapter titled "The Dignity of the Iceberg", and analysed for its suggestiveness, we can look at it again for its stylistic effects:

> The forest of oak trees on the mountain beyond the town was gone. The forest had been green in the summer when we had come into the town but now there were the stumps and the broken trunks and the ground torn up, and one day at the end of the fall when I was out where the oak forest had been I saw a cloud coming over the mountain. It came very fast and the sun went a dull yellow and then everything was grey and the sky was covered and the cloud came on down the mountain and suddenly we were in it and it was snow. The snow slanted across the wind, the bare ground was covered, the stumps of trees projected, there was snow on the guns and there were paths in the snow going back to the latrines behind the trenches (9).

Impressions and sensations are paraded in a systematic manner here. In addition, we are given a glimpse of the forest as it had been before the war and in a better season. It had been green in the summer. It was destroyed by the war in autumn. The fall would have damaged it anyway to some extent; but that would sprout new leaves and a new life in the next spring. But now the damage is permanent. The forest is dead now and there are only stumps like skeletal remains. Winter has commenced after the fall of the forest in the fall, and winter brings with it a shroud for the dead forest. This is shown in the play of nature without the narrator saying it in so many words. After giving us the impressions of stumps, broken trunks, and torn up ground, a cloud is shown in the sky coming over the mountain. It comes very fast and becomes larger and larger covering the whole sky and making everything grey. The sun seen through it goes a dull yellow. The narrator now finds that not only he but everyone is in it: the predominance of the liquid consonants, 'm', 'n', 'r' and 'l', making the impressions move fast, and the alliteration in 'broken trunks' and 'ground torn up' and 'dull yellow' assists in this movement. The singular 'I' yields place to the plural 'we' as the subjective vision of a single cloud becomes widespread snowfall covering everybody and everything.

As the image is extended, we find the snow slanting in the wind and covering the guns and the entire field of operations. The shroud of snow covers the battlefields, silences the guns, and declares a truce ordered by nature. Later, Henry and his friend look out at the snow and know it is all over for the year. Not only the forest but also the year and the fighting are dead for the time being.

The sequence of impressions is the structure of this picture which has a hidden metaphor. This is an extra metaphorical dimension, which is not explicit in the passage but subtly suggested as the narrator presents things truthfully as he sees them.

In Chapter VI of *In our Time*, a pain-stricken soldier in a trench, under heavy bombardment, makes the following prayer:

> While the bombardment was knocking the trench to pieces at Fossalta, he lay very flat and sweated and prayed. 'Oh Jesus Christ, get me out of here. Dear Jesus, Please get me out. Christ, please, please, please, Christ. If

> you'll only keep me from getting killed I'll do anything you say. I believe in you and I'll tell everybody in the world that you are the only thing that matters. Please, please, dear Jesus.... he did not tell the girl he went upstairs with at the *Villa* Rossa about Jesus. And he never told anybody.

The soldier under bombardment is cowardly and selfish. He does not want to die and prays to Jesus to save him. He prays for himself and promises Jesus that he will do whatever Jesus says and that he will tell everybody in the world that only Jesus matters. He is saved, but conveniently forgets his promises. He never tells anybody about Jesus later. The repetition in the prayer is necessitated by his anxiety and the gun fire. The sentences are simple imperative sentences of request and prayer and promise.

Now look at Henry's prayer for Catherine at the hospital:

> ... Everything was gone inside of me. I did not think. I could not think. I knew she was going to die and I prayed that she would not. Don't let her die. Oh, God, please don't let her die. I'll do anything for you if you won't let her die. Please, please, dear God, don't let her die. Dear God, don't let her die. Please, please, please don't let her die. God, please make her not die. I'll do anything you say if you don't let her die. You took the baby but don't let her die—that was all right but don't let her die. Please, please, dear God, don't let her die (254).

Like the soldier in the trench, Henry's prayer is repetitive and mechanical. He knows that Catherine is going to die and he prays hoping against hope. He cannot think; so great is his anxiety that he says the same thing again and again, using 'please' nine times.

Henry of *A Farewell to Arms*, unlike the panic-stricken soldier in the trench, is mature as a human being and has learnt that love makes one transcend selfish feelings. He prays for Catherine, not for himself. He has imbibed the priest's teaching on love that when one loves one wishes to do things for others and sacrifice oneself for others if necessary.

The impressionistic method of writing suits a situation like the Caporetto retreat very well. The retreat of the Italian army with its vehicles, weapons and troops is also joined by frightened civilians deserting their villages in carts and on foot with their belongings:

> In the night many peasants had joined the column from the roads of the country and in the column there were carts loaded with household goods; there were mirrors projecting up between mattresses, and chickens and ducks tied to carts. There was a sewing machine on the cart ahead of us in the rain. They had saved the most valuable things. On some carts the women sat huddled from the rain and others walked beside the carts keeping as close to them as they could. There were dogs now in the column keeping under the wagons as they moved along (154).

The description is realistic and kinetographic. It is like the camera moving from one object to another recording impression after impression—the peasants moving with their precious possessions like mirrors, mattresses, sewing machines, birds and beasts, the dogs under the wagons, chickens and ducks tied to the carts revealing the possessive nature of peasants, who are keen on saving not only their lives but their little possessions.

DEPICTION OF SENSATIONS

Hemingway excels in depicting sensations, ordinarily difficult to describe, like the feel of being hit by a trench mortar or the feel of sexual orgasm. The following is a depiction of how Henry almost dies when a trench mortar explodes in their dugout:

> Through the other noise I heard a cough, then came the chuh-chuh-chuh—then there was a flash, as a blast-furnace door is swung open, and a roar that started white and went red and on and on in a rushing wind. I tried to breathe but my breath would not come and I felt myself rush boldly out of myself and out and out and out and all the time bodily in the wind. I went out

> swiftly, all of myself and I knew I was dead and it had all been a mistake to think you just died. Then I floated, and instead of going on I felt myself slide back. I breathed and I was back (46).

Henry's sensations in the trench as the gun fire opens and the mortar shell explodes close to him are vividly described. As he is in the trench crouched, he cannot see the flash at the mouth of the gun but hears the chuh-chuh sound and when the mortar shell explodes close to him, it is like the door of a blast-furnace suddenly opening with a blinding light first white and then red, followed by a deafening roar. Then the feel of death as his soul rushes out of his body and floats for a while in the air. The eerie experience of watching his inert body for a while from above and then a more eerie experience of slipping back into it are described in a striking manner. The sensations are imparted, through a skilful use of words, to the reader.

But the above is the narrator's own experience, and it is always easier to describe one's own experience than to describe another person's experience, and Hemingway does the latter also in a remarkably effective manner. After his near-death experience, he hears some one screaming 'Mamma mia! Oh, mamma mia!' It was Passini, whose legs are smashed by the explosion, one leg completely gone, and the other, held by tendons and part of the trouser, twitching and jerking. Henry describes Passini's agony as follows:

> He bit his arm and moaned, 'oh mamma mia, mamma mia', then, 'Dio ti salvi, Maria. Dio ti salvi, Maria; Oh Jesus shoot me Christ shoot me, Mamma mia, mamma mia, oh purest lovely Mary shoot me. Stop it. Stop it. Stop it. Oh Jesus lovely Mary stop it. Oh oh oh oh', then choking, 'Mamma mamma mia.' Then he was quiet biting his arm, the stump of his leg twitching (47).

The capitalization indicates a sudden spasm or heightening of pain leading to the voice rising to a scream of pain, and the absence of punctuation shows the continuation of pain until another spasm convulses him. The unbearable nature of the spasm is indicated by the majority of the capitalized words being 'Jesus', 'Christ', and 'Mary'. Passini's occasional lapse into his mother tongue, Italian, the involuntary twitching of the stump of his leg, and the biting of the arm make this picture of unbearable pain complete.

His depiction of sensations during nights of drunken debauchery can be seen from the following passage in *A Farewell to Arms*:

> ... when the room whirled and you needed to look at the wall to make it stop, nights in bed, drunk, when you knew that that was all there was, and the strange excitement of waking and not knowing who it was with you, and the world all unreal in the dark and so exciting that you must resume again unknowing and not caring in the night, sure that this was all and all and all and not caring (14).

The drunken man's feelings during a night of sensual pleasures, the vague sensations, the unreality of it all and the repetition of 'all and all and all' express this experience excellently.

Hemingway's depiction of sexual orgasm is a daring attempt. The sensation, which is mainly a nerve-related phenomenon difficult of clear comprehension and description, is described in *For Whom the Bell Tolls*. For Maria whose eyes were tight closed against the sun and against everything, "everything was red, orange, gold-red from the sun on the closed eyes and it all was that colour, all of it, the filling, the possessing, the having, all of that colour, all in a blindness of that colour" (159). Here Hemingway does not appear to be on sure ground for this is a woman's orgasm, which is beyond Hemingway's experience. He links it with the colours in her closed eyes and does not sound quite convincing. Dorothy Hollis's masturbation in *To Have and Have Not* is described better with the aid of repetition and the shift between the pronouns 'I', 'he' and 'you' (245-246). Still it is like the masculine experience rather than the feminine one. But Hemingway sounds more convincing when he depicts Jordan's orgasm in *For Whom the Bell Tolls*:

> For him it was a dark passage which led to nowhere, then to nowhere, then again to nowhere, once again to nowhere, always and forever to nowhere, heavy on the elbows in the earth to nowhere, dark, never any end to nowhere, hung on all time always to unknowing nowhere, this time and again for always to nowhere, now not to be borne once again always and to nowhere, now beyond all bearing up, up, up and into nowhere, suddenly, scaldingly, holdingly all nowhere gone and time absolutely still and they were both there, time having slopped and he felt the earth move out and away from under them (159).

The dark passage leading to nowhere which repeats itself over and over in keeping with the discharges, the trance-like state of the mind, the physical sensation of heaviness on the elbows lapsing into the mental sensation of the journey to nowhere, the grammatical irregularity and the verbal incoherence work together to express the sensation.

STYLE AND POINT OF VIEW

The passages quoted above demonstrate how style is linked up with the character's consciousness. Style is related to point of view and is determined by it in good fiction. The style of Mark Twain's novel, *The Adventures of Huckleberry Finn*, is determined by the fact that Huck is the narrator. Anything except his own dialect in the mouth of Huck would be preposterous. The following passage from "Up in Michigan" included in *The Fifth Column and the First Forty-Nine Stories* illustrates this truth:

> Liz liked Jim very much. She liked it the way he walked over from the shop and often went to the kitchen door to watch for him to start down the road. She liked it about his mustache. She liked it about how white his teeth were when he smiled. She liked it very much that he didn't look like a blacksmith. She liked it how much D.J. Smith and Mrs. Smith liked Jim. One day she found that she liked it the way the hair was black on his arms and how white they were above the tanned line when he

> washed up in the wash basin outside the house. Liking that made her feel funny (179).

It is not merely the magic formula of repetition that demands our attention here. The story is told from the point of view of Liz Coates whose consciousness is central to its interest. Liz liked Jim and many things about him. If anybody asked her whether she loved him she would not be able to answer. She did not know it herself. Her liking was her feeling. A girl like Liz could not be expected to think in precise terms. She felt in a certain way about Jim and that feeling was funny. The writer repeats the word "like" effectively, and keeps track of her consciousness as it registers the different impressions concerning Jim one by one leading to the final impression that it "made her feel funny". The sum total of all these impressions is that the thought or sight of Jim gives Liz a pleasurable feeling. But Hemingway does not summarize it in this way, but dramatizes her consciousness so that we may be there with him watching it.

People generally do not think in precise or complex terms, but in simple vague terms like Liz liking several things about Jim or Henry thinking and talking about whisky as in the following passage from *A Farewell to Arms*:

> I would have to tell them not to put ice in the whisky. Let them bring the ice separately. That way you could tell how much whisky there was and it would not suddenly be too thin from the soda. I would get a bottle of whisky and have them bring ice and soda. That was the sensible way. Good whisky was very pleasant. It was one of the pleasant parts of life.
> 'What are you thinking darling?'
> 'About whisky'
> 'What about whisky?'
> 'About how nice it is' (237-238).

Words like 'nice', 'pleasant' and 'fine' are not precise in meaning but they convey a sense of well-being and most people prefer such words in day-to-day life.

DIALOGUE

The principle of verbal economy and understatement and the use of colloquial speech rhythms control Hemingway's dialogue. The old practice of underlining the intent or emotion or intonation of the speaker was discarded even by Mark Twain and Henry James. Hemingway carries this process to its logical conclusion making the dialogue completely dramatic with no commentary from the author except where it is absolutely necessary. The verb most commonly used is "said". Words indicative of intention or emotion are scrupulously avoided.

Hemingway's dialogues speak of the author's sensitive ear for the accents, inflexions, mannerisms, and emotional connotations of human speech. As Philip Young says in *Ernest Hemingway: A Reconsideration*, they give "an illusion of reality that, in its completeness, reality itself does not give" (205). Just as art, which is an imitation of life, is at the same time more than a mere imitation, dialogue in a work of art also is more than a mere imitation of human conversation while being basically an imitation of it. The important thing is the illusion the artist creates in his fictional world of people talking, for which the conversation should be convincing. According to Sam Boal's account quoted by John Atkins in *The Art of Ernest Hemingway*, Hemingway, after finishing his day's work, read it over to anyone who can be pressed into service—either his wife or a guest—asking now and then "That sound right? Hit your ear right? People talk that way?" (67). Henry James's motto, "Dramatize, Dramatize", is, perhaps, nowhere illustrated better than in Hemingway's fiction. In the following passage from *A Farewell to Arms*, Henry and Catherine have just had their dinner, and the trivial conversation hides the tension in their minds under the surface:

> The waiter came and took away the things. After a while we were very still and we could hear the rain. Down below on the street a motor car honked.
>
> 'And always at my back I hear
> Time's winged chariot hurrying near',
>
> I said.

> 'I know that poem', Catherine said. 'It's by Marvell. But it's about a girl who wouldn't live with a man.'
>
> ....
>
> '... How often will you write?'
>
> 'Every day. Do they read your letters?'
>
> 'They can't read English enough to hurt any.'
>
> 'I'll make them very confusing', Catherine said.
>
> 'But not too confusing.'
>
> 'I'll make them a little confusing.'
>
> 'I'm afraid we have to start to go.'
>
> 'All right, darling.'
>
> 'I hate to leave our fine house.'
>
> 'So do I.'
>
> 'But we have to go.'
>
> 'All right. But we're never settled in our home very long.'
>
> 'We will be.'
>
> 'I'll have a fine home for you when you come back.'
>
> 'Maybe I'll be back right away.'
>
> 'Perhaps you'll be hurt just a little in the foot.'
>
> 'Or the lobe of the ear.'
>
> 'No. I want your ears the way they are.'
>
> 'And not my feet?'
>
> 'Your feet have been hit already.'
>
> 'We have to go, darling. Really.'
>
> 'All right. You go first' (122-123).

They are in a hotel room and very happy as they are together for a while, which has become a rare luxury. This has become their home in the same way as Henry's room in the hospital. "My room in the hospital had been our own home and this room was our home too in the same way" (121). Their's is a story of love in the time of war. She is going to have a baby and he is going to the front after his discharge from the hospital. They are deeply in love and the impending separation causes an unbearable agony to both of them. The dialogue sounds light-hearted, but we get a sense of the undercurrent of tension.

The clues to the underlying tension could be seen in their being very still for some time—so still that they could hear the rain in that hotel room where all the sounds and sights of the outside world are shut out. Then they hear a car honking and that prompts him to quote from Marvell. The car honking is like Time's winged chariot hurrying near from behind trying to overtake him—like an alarm bell chasing him, and warning him of approaching disaster. She remembers that the poem is about a girl who *would not* live with a man. But she is a girl who *cannot* live with a man because of powerful factors. These are the thoughts and fears in their minds when they are very still. For him it is the call of duty driving him to the front and for her it is the baby in her womb already three months old.

But all these anxieties are muted and when he musters courage and asks her where she will have the baby, she parries the question and diverts the topic so that they talk about irrelevant things but central to this irrelevant conversation is their painful reluctance to part with each other ('I hate to leave our fine house'/ 'So do I').

Thus Hemingway gives us a feeling of the characters' emotions without explicitly stating them or describing them, leaving it to us to dig them out.

FOREIGN IDIOM

The locale for most of Hemingway's fiction is a foreign country. In *The Sun Also Rises*, it is partly France and partly Spain; in *A Farewell to Arms*, it is mostly Italy and partly Switzerland; in *To Have and Have Not,* it is Cuba and the Gulf Stream; in *For Whom the Bell Tolls*, it is Spain; in *Across the River and into the Trees*, it is Italy; in *The Old Man and the Sea*, it is Cuba and the Gulf Stream. Many of his short stories have a foreign setting. Hemingway gives the reader the feel of the country where the action takes place by a liberal use of foreign words and phrases.

In *A Farewell to Arms,* Henry is called *Tenante*. During the Caporetto retreat, the Italian soldiers throw a sprinkle of Italian into the dialogue:

> 'Tenante? Who's a Tenante? A *basso gli ufficiali*! Down with the officers!'
>
> ....
>
> 'If the war is over it makes no difference', Piani said. 'But I don't believe it's over. It's too good that it should be over.'
>
> 'We'll know pretty soon', I said.
>
> 'I don't believe it's over. They all think it's over but I don't believe it.'
>
> '*Evviva la pace*!' a soldier shouted out. 'We're going home' (171).

Foreign language, even though its English translation is supplied, gives us the feel of a foreign land. The passage given above is only a sample.

During the Caporetto retreat, Henry has a long free-associative dream-like chain of thought and talks with Catherine loudly forgetting that she is not there.

> 'You talked out aloud', Piani said.
>
> 'I was having a dream in English', I said (154).

We are given to understand that all the dialogues are in Italian for Henry is in Italy but his dreams are in English. Henry uses only Italian except when he speaks with Catherine—a native English speaker speaking with another native English speaker.

THE TWO STYLES

Hemingway's style is a highly controlled style—the result of rigorous training and discipline. But there is a duality about this style, one strand of which is a clipped, staccato type of prose, while the other rests mainly on literary allusions harking back nostalgically to the Elizabethans, for the most part, and the method is Eliotean, evoking the mood or the emotion associated with the quotation employed. The best example for this kind of style is the passage from *A Farewell to Arms*, cited and analysed in a masterly way by Charles R. Anderson:

> The column of vehicles did not move but the troops kept passing alongside. It was still raining hard and I thought some of the stops in the movement of the column might

> be from cars with wet wiring. More likely they were from horses or men going to sleep. Still, traffic could tie up in cities when everyone was awake. It was the combination of horse and motor vehicles. They did not help each other any. The peasants' carts did not help much either. Those were a couple of fine girls with Barto: A retreat was no place for two virgins. Real virgins. Probably very religious. If there were no war we would probably all be in bed. In bed I lay me down my head. Bed and board. Stiff as a board in bed. Catherine was in bed now between two sheets, over her and under her. Which side did she sleep on? Maybe she wasn't asleep: Maybe she was lying thinking about me. Blow, blow, ye western wind. Well, it blew and it wasn't the small rain but the big rain down that rained. It rained all night. You knew it rained down that rain. Look at it. Christ, that my love were in my arms and I in my bed again. That my love Catherine. That my sweet love Catherine down might rain. Blow her again to me. Well, we were in it. Everyone was caught in it and the small rain would not quiet it. 'Good night, Catherine', I said out aloud. 'I hope you sleep well. If it's too uncomfortable, darling, lie on the other side', I said. 'I'll get you some cold water. In a little while it will be morning and then it won't be so bad. I'm sorry he makes you so uncomfortable. Try to go to sleep, sweet (153-154).

Anderson sees three advantages in this dream sequence: (1) an escape from war at least in spirit, (2) the stylistic freedom from soldier-talk and a change of pace into tender, allusive and lyrical language, and (3) a justification, through sprung syntax and free association of ideas, of the abandonment of the logic of prose for the indirection and symbolism of poetry. But the amazing feature of this piece of writing, which Anderson misses, is its rhythm—the perfectly natural way in which the stream of consciousness flows from wakeful action to drowsiness first and then into sleep and dream and then into a dream within a dream and back to wakefulness again. Henry's thought of traffic deadlocks leads him to think of horses and motor vehicles; horses make him think of peasants carts; that leads him to think of the two girls, obviously peasant girls; and then he thinks of their virginity which leads to religion in a sleepy man's free-associative logic. He is, really, swiftly sliding into sleep now, and religion brings to his mind part of the child's prayer before sleep, "I lay me down." The prayer brings on the idea of bed, which is associated with board, both of which, on account of their association with 'home', lead to sexual yearnings. Then the two girls and Aymo's words, "No danger of—" and "No place for—", and the older girl stiffening away when he (Henry) touches her, all together make 'stiff as a board in bed'. Here, Anderson thinks that the board becomes stiffened into a phallic symbol of his longing for Catherine (43). Now Henry thinks of Catherine, if she is sleeping or thinking about him. In the twilight area between a drowsy, dreamy state preceding sleep and actual sleep and dream there is a lyrical gush in his heart. Anderson refers to the direct quotation from the anonymous Sixteenth Century lyric, "The Lover in Winter Plaineth for Spring",

> O western wind, when wilt thou blow
> That the small rain down can rain?
> Christ, that my love were in my arms
> And I in my bed again!

And to the lullaby in Tennyson's 'Princess' containing the lines,

> Sweet and low, sweet and low
> Wind of the western sea,
> ....
> Blow him again to me (43-45).

The pronoun is changed from "him" to "her" to suit the context. Anderson also calls attention to the traditional medieval symbol of Christ as the gentle rain and the distinction made in the dream-sequence between the "big rain" symbolizing the general destruction of war and the "small rain" plaguing their love without damping it. His yearning for his beloved, "that my love Catherine down might rain", reminds us of the mythological story of Zeus visiting Danae in a shower of gold.

But "Blow, blow, ye western wind" also seems to be an allusion to the song, "Blow, blow, thou winter wind" in Shakespeare's *As You Like It* (Act II, sc. vii, ll. 174-190). The song is associated with the Senior Duke and his courtiers living a hard life in exile, away from their homes and families, in the forest of Arden. The emotion is nostalgia like Henry's. The theme of the song, "Most friendship is feigning, most loving mere folly", is not borne out by the realities of the situation in the play, and so is it contradicted or inverted in Henry's case. Hemingway uses the first line as an objective correlative to evoke a mood of nostalgia—a longing for board, bed, and Catherine. From this semi-conscious dream-state he slips into a real dream in which his progress from a mere physical longing for Catherine to an unselfish affection and concern for her and the child in her womb is seen. This parallels not only his progress of a similar nature in the story but, in some measure, the progress of the Hemingway hero from erotic love to agape.

This lyrical interlude is locked in the arms of the bare, well-whittled, impressionistic depiction of the Caporetto retreat. Its lyricism does not spoil the rhythm of the passage in anyway but is perfectly in keeping with it. The rhythm is not merely logical but verbal in that it is not only the thoughts but words that lead the reader from sentence to sentence as in "we would probably all be in bed. In bed I lay me down my head. Bed and board. Stiff as a board in bed." But monotony is avoided by switching over to conventional sentences in Henry's talk with Catherine. Still the language continues to be tender and romantic until the dream is broken by Piani's expletive:

> I was asleep all the time, she said. You've been talking in your sleep. Are you all right?
> Are you really there?
> Of course, I'm here. I wouldn't go away. This doesn't make any difference between us.
> You are so lovely and sweet. You wouldn't go away in the night, would you?
> Of course, I wouldn't go away. I'm always here. I come whenever you want me.
> '______', Piani said. 'They've started again' (154).

The conventional language marks the transition from the romantic, lyrical style to the hard-boiled realistic style.

The two styles can be distinguished as separate entities in the first two novels, *The Sun Also Rises* and *A Farewell to Arms*, in which the contrapuntal theme is most pronounced. Irony is the main tone of the style as well as the theme of these two novels indicating the gap between incongruities. After Hemingway's African Safari and the publication of *Green Hills of Africa*, irony gradually yields place to paradox, and the prose aspires to the condition of poetry as the protagonist progresses from sex and violence to love and compassion.

8

Dynamics of Narration

THE STRUCTURE

The central theme of *A Farewell to Arms* is based on "A Very Short Story" of *In our Time*, which deals with a wartime affair between a wounded soldier and a Red Cross nurse. This story is based on Hemingway's own experience in Italy. The Red Cross nurse was Agnes Von Kurowsky, an American of Polish ancestry. Hemingway tells Hotchner thus:

> What happened between the Red Cross nurse and me is pretty much as I wrote it in "A Very Short Story.' Who really had the Caesarian was Pauline. Happened while I was writing *Farewell* in Kansas city. So that's part of Catherine; and Hadley is part of Catherine. But the Red Cross nurse was most of Catherine, plus some things that were of no woman I had ever known (104).

The novel is a development of the theme of "separate peace" (Chapter VI) and the theme of a soldier's religion (Chapter VII), which flank "A Very Short Story" on either side in *In our Time*. The basic structure of *A Farewell to Arms* can be seen in Chapter VI, "A Very Short Story", and Chapter VII of *In our Time* taken together. In Chapter VI, Nick, who is wounded in the spine, sits against the wall of the church and tells his friend Rinaldi: "*Senta Rinaldo; Senta*. You and me we've made a separate peace.... We're not patriots." The machine gun fire in the street explains the pledge by providing the relevant background. The twisted bedstead and the damaged house symbolize a ruined love and a ruined home. Nick becomes

Frederic Henry of *A Farewell to Arms*, and Rinaldi is split into Rinaldi and Catherine Barkley in the novel. It is with Catherine that Frederic Henry makes a separate peace, and bids farewell to arms by deserting the army, which is an unpatriotic act. In the novel, it is Rinaldi who introduces Henry to Catherine. In "A Very Short Story", the love affair between wounded Nick and the Red Cross nurse, Luz, is presented. Luz is Catherine's counterpart in the story. The love affair is shortlived as in the novel. Nick is forsaken by Luz, who breaks off her engagement with Nick in a letter. But, in the novel, Catherine dies in child-birth at the end. In both the cases, a farewell to the arms of love is indicated along with a farewell to arms.

Chapter VII of *In our Time* bears a close resemblance to the last chapter of *A Farewell to Arms*. The soldier (could be Nick), whose trench is under heavy bombardment, prays desperately:

> Oh Jesus Christ get me out of here. Dear Jesus, please get me out. Christ, please, please, please, Christ. If you'll only keep me from getting killed, I'll do anything you say. I believe in you and I'll tell everybody in the world that you are the only thing that matters. Please, please, dear Jesus.

He never tells anybody about it afterwards, and his religion is shortlived. In the novel, when Catherine is on her death-bed, Henry prays desperately and that is the only time he is found praying in the novel. The prayer runs very much like that in Chapter VII of *In our Time*; only Henry prays for Catherine and not for himself here:

> Oh, God, please don't let her die. I'll do anything for you if you won't let her die. Please, please, please don't let her die. God please make her not die. I'll do anything you say if you don't let her die. You took the baby but don't let her die. That was all right but don't let her die. Please, please, dear God, don't let her die (254).

The protagonist suffering a serious injury in the battlefield (Chapter VI of *In our Time*), the love affair with a Red Cross nurse in the hospital ("A Very Short Story"), a desperate prayer by the protagonist in the end (Chapter VII of *In our Time*)—this is the basic structure of the novel. It is significant that "A Very Short Story", which alone can be taken as representing the central episode of *A Farewell to Arms* in a way, is flanked on either side by machine gun fire and bombardment.

The opening chapter of the novel which, as Carlos Baker rightly points out, "helps to establish the dominant mood (which is one of doom)" (94), concludes with a significant reference to the rain which is associated with the death of "only seven thousand" men in the army. The opening chapter describes the marching troops, a motorcade, and the march of seven thousand soldiers out of the world owing to cholera. The picture is one of a passing generation versus the abiding earth, represented here by rain. In the last chapter, as Catherine moves fast towards death, Henry reflects on the inexorable 'They', who "threw you in and told you the rules and the first time they caught you off base they killed you" (252). He remembers the tragic episode of the ants which died in a camp fire. The scenes describing Catherine's labour and suffering alternate with these reflections and the flux of life reflected in the crowded café where several card games are going on and saucers are piled up on the table, and all the while it rains outside. When the focus is lifted from the story, which is indicated by the narrator-protagonist turning off the light, we are made conscious of the rain in the background.

When the different strands which go into the making of the novel are taken into consideration, a complex pattern emerges with love, war, and death as the major themes. According to Philip Young in his *Ernest Hemingway: A Reconsideration*, the courses of love and war in the novel run exactly parallel so that in the end we feel we have read one story, not two. In his affair with the war, Henry goes through six phases: desultory participation, serious action, wound, recuperation in Milan, and retreat leading to desertion. His relationship with Catherine undergoes six precisely corresponding stages: trifling sexual affair, actual love, conception, confinement in the Alps, trip to the hospital and death (93). M.K. Naik's question, "why, for instance, if Professor Young is right, should the author have divided his novel into five books?" (79) is interesting. Naik rightly sees a special thematic significance in this division of the novel. But the fact that the author has a certain plan does not invalidate the critic's interpretation which may not agree with the author's scheme, and, so the importance of Young's interpretation cannot be belittled.

A close look at Young's interpretation reveals the two parallel stories as those of Henry and Catherine also. The war story is Henry's and the love story is Catherine's, in a broad sense, since the different phases from desultory participation to desertion pertain to Henry while the six corresponding stages from trifling love affair to death through conception and confinement, primarily, pertain to Catherine. War is the connecting link between the two, as it brings Henry and Catherine together. Henry stands for war and its different facets including desertion and escape from execution, while Catherine, with her attitude of supreme surrender to love, is the very personification of love. It is again the ancient story of Ares, the Greek god of war, and Aphrodite, the Greek goddess of love, being in love and trapped in the golden net made by Hephaestus, the wrathful god of fire and husband of Aphrodite burning with jealousy and revengefulness. Like them Henry and Catherine are also trapped in the end.

The opening chapter is a prefatory one, and the story actually begins with Chapter II. The first book deals with war and ends with Henry's wound and hosptalization. Whatever love is there in this book is only incidental, though of germinal importance. But, in the second book, this love develops into a major theme and war is only in the distant background. Only Henry hears its rumblings at his back as he quotes Marvell later:

> And always at my back I hear
> Time's winged chariot hurrying near (122).

In the third book, war reappears as the major theme again and Henry quickly passes through retreat, desertion, and escape from execution by the Carabinieri. The farewell to arms is complete here. In the fourth book, love comes to the fore once again and leads to the escapade to Switzerland, and war recedes to the distant background. In the fifth book, the trap closes, and death cuts off the lover's retreat to an idyllic life, even as the Carabinieri cut off the retreat of many officers including Henry to a safer life in the third book. The story comes full circle with Henry, once again alone, with nothing left, coming back to the 'I' at the beginning of the story, and the rain ceaselessly pattering all the while. Thus the novel has a circular structure.

Edmund Wilson reports, in *The Wound and the Bow*, Hemingway's remark that *A Farewell to Arms* is his *Romeo and Juliet* (180). The comparison holds good only with reference to the tragic story of love set in an atmosphere charged with hostilities, and the division of the novel into five books corresponding to the five acts of a tragedy. But the analogy cannot be carried too far. The hostilities have little to do with Catherine's death, which is brought about by the biological problems of childbirth. Henry does not kill himself in the end. The whole situation in *A Farewell to Arms* is different from that in *Romeo and Juliet.* But as a love story with a tragic end, it makes us hark back to other immortal love stories in legend and classical literature like Marlowe's "Hero and Leander", Sir Walter Scott's "Lochinvar", and Keats's *The Eve of St. Agnes*—all of which are tragic love stories set in a climate of hostilities.

THE USE OF IRONY

There is a strange irony in Henry bidding farewell to arms and running to the arms of his beloved, where he expects to find security and comfort, but soon finding himself bidding farewell to these arms also. Henry bids farewell to what he hates most and then to what he loves most too. Henry's belief that he has gained a heavenly happiness turns out to be a mere illusion for the gain becomes a loss and what he really gains is a dreadful misery and sad loneliness. This basic tragic irony makes itself manifest in the novel in a variety of ways and situations. The ironic tone is set in the opening chapter in which are described the troops with the boxes of cartridges bulging forward under their capes, marching "as though they were six months gone with child", carrying death under their capes, and the little king, whose face could not be seen as he sits between two generals in the car, seeing for himself how things are going. The ironic understatement that "only seven thousand" men in the army had died in the winter before the cholera was checked concludes the opening chapter. Then follow scenes of priest-baiting, which are full of ironic banter. Henry wishes to go to Abruzzi, during his leave, as desired by the priest, but goes instead to cities like Milan, Florence, Naples and Rome, where he drowns himself in sensual pleasures. Rinaldi speaks of his love for Catherine ("I will probably marry Miss Barkley") but Henry gets involved with her eventually. Rinaldi introduces Henry to Catherine but Henry wants to develop an affair with her. He plans a trifling affair but falls deeply in love with her later.

Henry is wounded while eating macaroni and cheese in the dug-out; the Red Cross officer whose business is to receive the wounded is one of the first to be wounded, and to crown it all, he is decorated for bravery. The following is the dialogue between Rinaldi and Henry in the hospital ward where Henry lies wounded:

> '... you will be decorated. They want to get you the medaglia d'argento but perhaps they can get only the bronze.'
>
> 'What for?'
>
> 'Because you were gravely wounded. They say if you can prove you did any heroic act you can get the silver. Otherwise it will be the bronze. Tell me exactly what happened. Did you do any heroic act?'
>
> 'No', I said. 'I was blown up while we were eating cheese.'

In the above dialogue there is an unexpressed ironic comment, which can be read between the lines, on how prizes are awarded and honours conferred in the world. Henry is wounded while eating cheese and macaroni, but is decorated for bravery in the battlefield. The deserving go unrecognized and unhonoured while the undeserving are honoured and rewarded in this world, sometimes. The irony underlying this can be seen in the dialogue between Henry and Rinaldi.

During the Caporetto retreat Henry shoots a sergeant, who is not his subordinate, for desertion. Later, he himself is all but shot for the same crime by the battle police and manages to escape from execution by jumping into the Tagliamento (312-313). E.M. Halliday, in his essay, "Hemingway's Ambiguity: Symbolism and Irony", points out this and some other examples to underline the importance of irony in Hemingway's fiction. Count Greffi and Henry discuss religion and devotion drinking champagne. Count Greffi has been perpetually waiting for devotion which does not come to him, while Henry's devotion comes only at night. Henry and Catherine plan to "go to sleep at exactly the same moment" but Henry is awake for a long time after Catherine goes to sleep, which is a dramatic irony wrapped in a dramatic correlative of what is going to befall them in the near future. Catherine going to sleep before Henry foreshadows her predecease before Henry's, though Henry and Catherine, in their intense love, swear that they cannot live without each other. The baby takes the place of war in the last book, and gives them a feeling as though something were hurrying them. The cosmic irony of all-consuming time is reflected in the image of time's winged chariot, which overtakes not only Henry and Catherine but all life, countries and continents, planets and stars, and galaxies. A dog noses at a refuse can in the hope of finding something to eat, but the refuse can refuses to offer anything but coffee grounds, dust, and dead flowers. The nurses are excited and call themselves lucky to see a Caesarian operation, as Catherine is struggling against death. Henry remembers how he thinks it a splendid chance to play the role of a Messiah and lift the log off the fire and save the ants, but throws a tin cup of water on the burning log of wood, which only steams the ants to death. Actually he wants to save the ants but, in his attempt to translate his intention into action, things go completely wrong and the opposite effect is achieved. Instead of giving life, he gives death to the ants. Then there is the final dramatic irony of devotion coming to Henry in the night but in a different sense and context.

Bill Gorton's bantering allusions to "irony" and "pity" have a relevance to this novel as much as to *The Sun Also Rises*, for both are conceived and executed in the tragic mould—*A Farewell to Arms* as a tragedy in five books corresponding to five acts, and *The Sun Also Rises* in three parts in the mould of the three-part tragedy of the Spanish bullfight. The ironic tone of the early chapters is gradually lost in the tragic irony of the narrator's story of which we become more and more conscious as the story advances. The emotional tension, which is associated mainly with war, is shifted to love in the last two books in which there is only a steady rise of it until Catherine's death at the end. The war-scenes alternate with the love-scenes, which provide relief from seriousness and tension, in the first three books. As this love-theme gains in emotional intensity in the last two books, the ironic tone fades away before the tragic irony of the lover's story, especially Henry's.

THE NARRATIVE PERSPECTIVE

The story is told in the first person by Frederic Henry in retrospect. There is a sad irony about the narration as he relives his memories. His early involvement with the war, his gradual separation from it, his total involvement with Catherine, and his final bereavement are skilfully indicated by the alternation of "I" and "We" in the narration. The first chapter being introductory, the actual narrative starts with the second chapter, the narrator appearing as "I", occasionally referring to his involvement by using "We" and "Us", sometimes using both "I" and "We" in the same sentences expressing his personal action as well as his involvement with his companions: "When I came back to the front we still lived in that town" (12).

In this novel, the first-person narrator knows his business thoroughly and every particular he mentions contributes to the exposition of the subject of love being clasped in the powerful arms of war, and both trapped together in the cruel mesh of fate. He does full justice, as narrator, to the parallel themes of war and love in both of which he is the protagonist. As he looks at his experiences by hindsight, the focus is on him in both the stories. The love-story is an elaboration of Brett's words, "It isn't all that you know" (*The Sun Also Rises*, 26); it stresses the fact that love is more than sex. Henry, the narrator, traces the growth of Henry, the protagonist (i.e. himself), from the whore houses and the "nights in bed drunk, when you know that that was all there was (14), to love, which is "a religious feeling" in Count Greffi's words (203). He traces the growth of the protagonist (himself) from active participation in war to desertion and a total break with war. Then he describes the protagonist's (his own) brief life of happiness with his beloved, which gives him a sense of security against all odds, when, suddenly, the tragic biological trap closes on them, depriving the narrator-protagonist, Henry, of that prop and comfort too. He is now left to face the world and his grief alone.

The bare, realistic prose of the war-story and the tender, romantic prose of the love-story combine to give us a tragic feeling towards the end. The same tightness of texture and concentration on the development of the subject as characterize *The Sun Also Rises* are in close evidence in this novel. This helps the writer give us a superior point of view revealing the tragic irony in the predicament of Henry and several other minor ironies all of which contribute to the main irony in the novel dealing with the farewell to the good arms as well as the bad arms, the killing arms and the comforting arms, the arms of hatred and the arms of love. It is not possible for the first-person narrator to be conscious of all these ironies which we notice as he is part of the story and is affected by the happenings. This gives us an objective point of view, which enables us to perceive the philosophical aspect of the story. The narrator's controlled presentation of his material "shows" rather than "tells" the story.

The first-person narration lends an immediacy to the narrative bouncing the reader into the belief that it all really happened to the narrator. The reader identifies himself with the first-person narrator, who transmits a complete sense of experience to the reader. A third-person narrative is distant from the reader, who cannot respond to it in the same measure as to a first-person narrative. In *A Farewell to Arms*, the first-person narrator recollects the events after a lapse of time and recounts them for us throwing in his reflections and comments now and then and the verbal and situational ironies become possible owing to this lapse of time. The narrator occasionally assumes a pensive tone giving us the impression that he has grown wise after the event, as in the following reflection of Henry's about the priest:

> He had always known what I did not know and what, when I learned it, I was always able to forget. But I did not know that then, although I learned it later (15).

Some passage of time is necessary after an experience to gain a proper perspective.

The first-person method of narration makes the narrative, tight, direct, and powerful. The first two novels of Hemingway, *The Sun Also Rises* and *A Farewell to Arms* have this virtue.

But this method has its limitations. As Percy Lubbock puts it, the narrative is "rounded by the bounds of the narrator's own personal experience" (257). But Hemingway more than makes up for this limitation by keeping an undeviating focus on Henry's story of love and war.

THE TIME OF ACTION AND THE TIME OF NARRATION

H.R. Stoneback in his excellent essay "'Lovers' Sonnets Turn'd to Holy Psalms': the Soul's Song of Providence, the Scandal of Suffering, and Love in *A Farewell to Arms*," calls the narrative Frederic Henry's "narrative meditation some years after the action, on certain key events which have shaped his life" (34).

Stoneback quotes James Nagel's view that the story was told in retrospect a decade after the action had taken place "for the purpose of coming to terms emotionally with the events." One of the time-indicators mentioned by Nagel is

Frederic Henry's brief reference to Babe Ruth that Babe Ruth was a pitcher *then*, at the time of action which implies that he *is not now*, at the time of telling. Another time-indicator in Nagel's argument is Henry's references to Count Greffi's age at two different times when he met him:

> Count Greffi was ninety-four years old .... He was living to be one hundred years old and played a smoothly fluent game of billiards that contrasted with his own ninety-four-year-old brittleness (196).

The references in the above passage are clear and specific. But they refer to the intervening six years between the last time he had played billiards with Count Greffi and now, and not to the time that has elapsed before the telling of the story, which makes it more than six years. Stoneback while questioning Nagel's theory of a decade's gap says:

> Doesn't a decade later seem rather late in the game for Frederic to be coming to terms with his experience? If it is that much later we might conclude that Frederic is a slow learner, or, he has been very busy, too busy to get around to telling this all-important story. Since there is no evidence to support these conclusions, and since the understated intensity of the suffering confirms that the narration, the need to tell the story, is more urgent than a time-lapse of a decade suggests, I would argue that the narration occurs, at the latest, about six years after the action (35-36).

Quite reasonable and cautious in that Stoneback uses 'about' avoiding preciseness. It might be a little more than six years after the action that the narration takes place. We need not be fussy about this. What is important is to remember that Henry tells the story in retrospect, a few years after the action.

9

Characters

In a dramatized narrative, characterization becomes integrated with the dynamics of form and its purpose is to contribute to the intensity, to the total effect of the narrative. A character is understood in a proper perspective only when we take into consideration how other characters see it to supplement our own assessment. The milieu in which Jake or Henry or Brett or Catherine or any other person is placed and what the seeing eye records concerning that person—this is how a character takes shape in the reader's mind, e.g. when Brett is first introduced in *The Sun Also Rises*, we learn about her only through the mechanics of dramatized narration and the narrator does not tell us anything about her by himself. All that he tells us is that a crowd of young men, some in shirt sleeves and some in jerseys come to the bar and "with them was Brett". Jake hears two of these young men talk with each other and remarks again: "And with them was Brett." He tells us that he was very angry and thus we get the feeling that she has associated with undesirable people. Cohn and Jake walk over to the bar when Brett also comes up and greets them. The narrator sees that she is standing, holding the glass. Then he finds that Robert Cohn is looking at her "as his compatriot must have looked when he saw the promised land" (22). Then he looks at Brett again and notices how damned good looking she is, in her slip-over jersey sweater and tweed skirt. Her hair is brushed back like a boy's. "She was built with curves like the hull of a racing yacht, and you missed none of it with that wool jersey" (22). Jake refers to the fine crowd she is with, and later, she says that she can drink in safety with that crowd. That it is a group of homosexuals is only left to our imagination and it is not only Brett's appearance but her character, her unconventionality, promiscuity, and brashness that comes out in this scene. Robert Cohn's romantic devotion and Jake's intimacy with Brett, which is responsible for his not noticing Brett's attractiveness until he sees Cohn's reaction, are also suggested here.

Frederic Henry's and Catherine's characters also unfold in the same way as a combination of our assessment and as others see them, treat them, and interact with them.

FREDERIC HENRY

If *The Sun Also Rises* opens with Robert Cohn, *A Farewell to Arms* opens with the priest. Both these characters, who are not the protagonists, help in the unfolding of the characters of the hero and the heroine. The priest, in particular, has a central role in the novel as the hero's spiritual guide and mentor in love, who opens up new horizons of the heart. In both the novels, we are misled into thinking initially that Cohn in *The Sun Also Rises* and the priest in *A Farewell to Arms* might be the protagonists of those novels but, later, learn that they are minor characters. But they are minor characters of considerable significance in that they contribute to our understanding of the protagonists.

The priest is the odd man out in the army mess. His religious and moral qualities mark him out as a different kind of person. People, who are different, are generally made fun of and sometimes, disliked. The priest, therefore, becomes the target of banter in the mess. The captain, in particular, cracks jokes at the expense of the priest, who suffers it all with a smile. The major, the captain, the lieutenant and others except Henry participate in this game and enjoy priest-baiting. The fact that Henry does not participate in this fun, and treats the priest with respect shows him in a different light—a notch above the others on the spiritual scale. It shows that Henry is not like the others in the unit and the mess. In spite of his frivolous attitude to love and Catherine, this little sign of spirituality makes his mind and heart fertile soil for the teaching of the priest: "When you love you wish to do things for. You wish to sacrifice for. You wish to serve." Henry's respect for the priest, his non-participation in priest-baiting, and his desire to go to the Abruzzi though he cannot fulfil this desire and, in fact, does the opposite by going to the cities and houses of sin, reveal him as a different type of person like the priest, though in a lesser degree than the latter. But his companions in the mess do not make fun of him as he appears to them like one of them—a person fond of the pleasures of the flesh, who goes to whore-houses and the pleasures of the city rather than the cold dry heights of Abruzzi.

The symbolism of the mountain versus plain is nowhere better expressed than in *A Farewell to Arms*. The first sentence of the novel establishes the mountains as the signifiers of the ideal—the goals to be reached or the heights to be attained: "In the late summer of that year we lived in a house in a village that looked across the river and plain to the mountains."

Henry may visit the whore-houses, but his mind is irresistibly drawn to the mountains or the snow-fall or the priest, that stand for the higher values:

> Later, below in the town, I watched the snow falling, looking out of the window of the bawdy-house, the house for officers, where I sat with a friend and two glasses drinking a bottle of Asti, and, looking out at the snow falling slowly and heavily, we knew it was all over for that year. Up the river the mountains had not been taken; ... my friend saw the priest .... The priest looked up. He saw us and smiled (9).

In spite of his affinity with the priest, Henry has a virile macho image in the early parts of the novel. He enjoys his camaraderie with other officers in the mess. He is accepted by them as one of them. They invite him to stay with their families at different ports of call. They suggest places where Henry can have sensual pleasures—Rome, Naples, Amalfi, Palermo and Capri. Only the priest advises the heights of Abruzzi. His friends think only of sexual pleasures for Henry at these places. When Henry returns from his leave, his colleagues ask him where he went and what he did. Henry boastfully reels off the names of the cities he visited—Milan, Florence, Naples, Rome, etc. They talk of beautiful girls, which prompts Rinaldi to refer to his love for Miss Barkley.

That night at the mess Henry sits next to the priest, who feels hurt that he (Henry) has not gone to the Abruzzi. Henry explains that he really wanted to go to the Abruzzi but one thing led to another and he finally went elsewhere. His higher mind wanted to go to the Abruzzi but his lower mind or basic instinct took him to the sinful cities. The priest, whose instinct is guided by the higher mind, understands spontaneously. Henry puts it thus:

> ... he understood that I had really wanted to go to the Abruzzi but had not gone and we were still friends, with many tastes alike, but with the difference between us. He had always known what I did not know and what, when I learned it, I was always able to forget. But I did not know that then, although I learned it later (15).

The priest understands the nature and mind of Henry. He knows with his uncanny spiritual insight that in his heart of hearts Henry wanted to go to the Abruzzi but the weakness of the flesh and the senses drew him to the places of sin. The dichotomy of the two minds—the lower mind guided by the senses and the higher mind which discriminates between right and wrong or good and bad—is presented here. Henry's higher mind wanted to do the right thing by going to the Abruzzi but his lower mind takes him to places where his sensual desires are fulfilled. People generally ignore the intimations which come from the higher mind and follow the urges of the lower mind. Henry also persuades himself that what he really wanted to do was what he was doing. Thus he exchanges war for love believing that he really wanted to abandon his duties as a soldier in favour of his love for Catherine. He deceives himself into believing that this is what he really wants. Henry makes a separate peace believing that he is tired of war. But the other characters carry on with their duties even though they are also tired of war. They endure discharging their duties unlike Henry and Catherine.

The separate peace fails even before Catherine dies. John Beversluis holds the view that Lewis's comment that Henry is relieved when Catherine dies reflects his fidelity to the text of the novel. The separate peace, according to Beversluis, brings emptiness and boredom. Henry comes to the realization, in Switzerland, that he and Catherine have little to talk about except their love, "Finally he can contain himself no longer and blurts out what had been smouldering just beneath the surface for sometime; he tells Catherine that his life used to be full, but that now he does not have a thing in the world (20-21).

But such outbursts are often the result of taut nerves and a state of tension and anxiety, and should not be taken at their face-value. Beversluis reconciles the contradictions thus:

> People often experience "mixed" and even "contrary" emotions. Why not Frederic Henry? True, he had grown weary of the separate peace, but he had loved Catherine too.... A hallowed tradition assures us that it is better to have loved and lost than never to have loved at all, that loving and being loved cannot fail to improve us, and that the wisdom thus gained is available in no other, less costly way (25).

Frederic Henry's story is one of love—an intense love that takes him towards 'peace' and 'home'. The names, 'Frederic' and 'Henry' are listed in the Roman Catholic version of *The Holy Bible*. Frederic is, there, described as 'peace-ruler' and Henry 'home-ruler'. *The Book of Saints*: *A Dictionary of Servants of God Canonized by the Catholic Church* (1921 edition), one of Hemingway's favourite sources, tells us about Saint Frederic, crusader against illegal marriages, and Saint Henry, warrior and man of peace, who retreated from the world and ill-fated marriage prospects (Stoneback, 38). Curiously enough, both are associated with ill-fated marriages. Frederick Henry's love-life with Catherine is illegal as they are not married and ill-fated as it ends in disaster. But both are saints, who have lent their names to the hero of the novel—

Frederic Henry. No wonder we have a protagonist, who is a devout catholic with an unwavering faith in the immortality of the soul. When he almost died in the explosion of the trench mortar, he describes the experience thus:

> I tried to breathe but my breath would not come and I felt myself rush bodily out of myself and out and out and out and all the time bodily in the wind. I went out swiftly, all of myself and I knew I was dead and it had all been a mistake to think you just died. Then I floated, and instead of going on I felt myself slide back. I breathed and I was back (46).

Henry's rushing out of himself, his going out of his body "all of himself", his statement that "it would be a mistake to think that you just died", are all unmistakable references to the immortality of the soul. Then he floated and felt himself slide back into his body. Henry floated and reentered his inert body. All the while he was alive and aware of what was happening; hence the statement that it would be a mistake to think that he 'just died' since he, as soul, has no death.

This is not to say that Henry has never thought about the soul and its immortality before his near-death experience. During their very first conversation, Catherine tells Henry about the death of her boyfriend:

> '... and then of course he was killed and that was end of it.'
>
> 'I don't know.'
>
> 'Oh, yes, she said. That's the end of it' (19).

In the above conversation, we find Henry an incomplete doubting believer, one who wants to believe but is not quite sure. But Catherine sounds like a sure and confident unbeliever.

When Henry comes under the influence of the priest, a complete, confident believer, his character undergoes a transformation. Besides, the priest is the shepherd of souls; he is the tutor for tyros like Henry; he is the instructor of the code to heroes like Henry. At meeting after meeting with the priest, Henry seems to like him more and more. The priest has a winsome smile and exercises a noble influence on Henry. Any smile is an expression of grace, and the priest is a man of God and his smile is bound to have a special power. Henry and his friend see the priest through the window of the mess. The priest sees them and *smiles*. When the captain teases him saying "priest today with girls", the priest *smiles* and blushes when the lieutenant praises a book titled *The Black Pig* and recommends it for Henry's reading. Henry smiles at him and the priest *smiles* back across the candlelight.

Later, the priest visits Henry at the hospital with a few gifts, and, when Henry asks him about the mess, he *smiles* and says that he is still a great joke. When the priest says that in his country a man may love God and it is not a dirty joke, Henry says he understands. The priest *smiles* and says, 'you understand, but you don't love God'. Now comes the psychological moment for the priest to drive home his teaching:

> 'You do not love Him at all?' he asked.
> 'I am afraid of Him in the night sometimes.'
> 'You should love Him.'
> 'I don't love much.'
> 'Yes', he said. 'You do. What you tell me about in the nights. That's not love. That is only passion and lust—when you love you wish to do things for. You wish to sacrifice for. You wish to serve.'
> 'I don't love.'
> 'You will. I know you will. Then you will be happy' (60).

The priest prophesies that Henry will love and know the true meaning of love. He tells Henry that what he has experienced so far is only passion and lust, and proceeds to teach him the meaning of love. This teaching is followed a little later by another smile and a pat on Henry's hand by the priest looks like Henry's initiation.

After this initiation Henry encounters fabulous forces, the first of which is the kind of love expounded by the priest, which transforms his personality, and then the massive Caporetto retreat followed by his arrest and escape from execution by the Carabinieri by a daring, adventurous swim, partly under water, and, later, as the biological trap closes in on him, another daring escapade by rowing in a boat on a stormy night into another country where he suffers the final blow in the form of Catherine's death.

We find his soul's progress through all these experiences as the narrative moves forward. After he receives the teaching on love, he is shifted to the American hospital in Milan, where he meets Catherine again. After their exchange of words of mutual love, Catherine leaves promising to come again and this is how Henry feels:

> God knows I had not wanted to fall in love with her. I had not wanted to fall in love with anyone. But God knows I had and I lay on the bed in the room of the hospital in Milan and all sorts of things went through my head .... (75).

What happens to Henry is totally unexpected and contrary to his wishes. What he did earlier in going to the cities and indulging in pleasures in the cities was contrary to his wish to go to the Abruzzi. Now what happens to him does not leave him any choice. He did not want to fall in love but he falls head and shoulders in love. During their second meeting he tries to kiss her and she slaps him. When they meet for the third time she thaws considerably and allows him to kiss her. She feels and acts romantic while he fakes love:

> 'You have been away a long time.'
> 'This is the third day. But I'm back now.'
> She looked at me. 'And you do love me?'
> 'Yes'.
> 'You did say you loved me, didn't you?'
> 'Yes', I lied. 'I love you.' I had not said it before (27).

He finds this meeting better than going to the whore-house, where the girls climb all over him:

> I knew I did not love Catherine Barkley nor had any idea of loving her. This was a game, like bridge, in which you said things instead of playing cards. Like bridge, you had to pretend you were playing for money or playing for some stakes (28).

Later, after his escape from the Carabinieri and his desertion from the army, he joins Catherine. He cannot bear even a moment's separation from her and feels extremely lonely when she is not present.

> ... and Catherine was not back yet. I lay down on the bed and tried to keep from thinking.
>
> When Catherine came back it was all right again....
>
> 'What's the matter, darling?'
>
> 'I don't know.'
>
> 'I know. You haven't anything to do. All you have is me and I go away.'
>
> 'That's true.'
>
> 'I'm sorry, darling. I know it must be a dreadful feeling to have nothing at all suddenly.'
>
> 'My life used to be full of everything', I said. 'Now if you aren't with me, I haven't a thing in the world.'
>
> 'But I will be with you. I was only gone for two hours....' (198).

Henry's remark that his life used to be full of everything once, but now he does not have anything in the world in the absence of Catherine could be examined from another angle and the perspective changes. His love for Catherine becomes so deep now that she is his whole world. Her absence for two hours makes him restless and anxious and, when she returns, he becomes all right again.

Just as Catherine says, "I want what you want. There isn't any me any more. Just what you want", Henry says, "My life used to be full of everything. Now if you aren't with me, I haven't a thing in the world." She is the whole world for him and he is the whole world for her. When one is absent, the other feels miserable. It is not necessarily his boredom that makes Henry speak that way as Lewis thinks.

During the conversation between the Count Greffi and Henry there are some significant statements. The Count remarks that the old only grow careful, not wise (202). The Count always expected to become devout, but devotion does not come to him.

> 'I had always expected to become devout. All my family died very devout. But somehow it does not come.'
>
> 'It's too early.'
>
> 'May be it's too late. Perhaps I have outlived my religious feeling.'
>
> 'My own comes only at night.'
>
> 'Then too you are in love. Do not forget that is a religious feeling' (203).

Love is a religious feeling, the priest's kind of love in particular. Love is God's manifestation in the world when you wish to do things for and sacrifice for another or serve others. In short, when there is no self-interest, love becomes exalted. It becomes a religious or spiritual feeling. The Count Greffi clarifies this for Henry. It is said that love is God. The highest form of devotion is love—love of God, which has no selfish interest. Henry has not yet reached that state but now Catherine is his religion.

Frederic Henry, the peace-ruler and the home-ruler, as his name signifies, wants the true love between himself and Catherine to lead to its logical conclusion of marriage. He repeatedly offers to marry Catherine, but Catherine, for whom love is not merely her religion but an end in itself, turns down his proposal. Even though they were not married in a religious or legal way, they were as good as married, if not more than married from a higher point of view, i.e. in terms of love and divine laws.

> I wanted to be really married but Catherine said that if we were they would send her away ...
>
> 'May be they wouldn't.'
>
> 'They would. They'd send me home and then we would be apart until after the war.'
>
> 'I'd come on leave.'
>
> 'You couldn't get to Scotland and back on a leave. What

> good would it do to marry now? We're really married. I couldn't be any more married.'
>
> 'I only wanted to for you.'
>
> 'There isn't any me. I'm you. Don't make up a separate me' (90).

Apart from the practical problems and the hurdles in the way of their marriage, the motivation for his desire to marry her and for her unwillingness should be understood. He wants to marry her because he does not want their child to be born outside the religious and legal framework of marriage. She does not care for marriage as her love is too great and too deep for marriage. She does not feel like a separate entity from him. In her case, it is total self-surrender— a merger of her individual self in him. From the following dialogue, which is a continuation of the one cited above, it becomes clear that religion means more to him than to her:

> 'There's no way to be married except by church or state. We're married privately. You see, darling, it would mean everything to me if I had any religion. But I haven't any religion.'
> 'You gave me the Saint Anthony.'
> 'That was for luck. Someone gave it to me.'
> 'Then nothing worries you ?'
> 'Only being sent away from you. You're my religion. You're all I've got.'
> 'All right. But, I'll marry you the day you say' (91).

Catherine has no religion other than Henry, but Henry takes religion seriously. The Saint Anthony is a religious icon for him, a religious talisman, while it is a charm for good luck for Catherine. He is ready to marry her on any day she likes.

Thus we find that Henry's love is, in some way, mixed up with religion. The priest's words seem to guide him all the while. Still he is not as philosophical and objective as the priest. He believes that people become gentle and Christian only in defeat. Somehow, in his mind, religion and gentleness are mixed up with defeat. He is defeatistic unlike the priest, for whom religion is a positive value which has little to do with victory or defeat. Their opposite viewpoints are brought out in the following discussion:

> '... I only think the Austrians will not stop when they have won a victory. It is in defeat that we become Christian.'
>
> 'The Austrians are Christians—except for the Bosnians.'
>
> 'I don't mean technically Christian. I mean like our Lord.'
>
> He said nothing.
>
> 'We are all gentler now because we are beaten. How would our Lord have been if Peter had rescued him in the Garden?'
>
> 'He would have been just the same.'
>
> 'I don't think so', I said.
>
> 'You discourage me', he said. 'I believe and I pray that something will happen. I have felt it very close' (139).

Henry sounds like a passive Christian in contrast with the priest, who is an active Christian. He believes that suffering and defeat lead to gentleness and Christianity and that Jesus is no exception, while the priest does not share that view. For him a Christian is a Christian in victory or in defeat, and Jesus would have remained the same even if he had escaped from crucifixion.

The discussions with the priest and the references to Jesus and prayer have a strong influence on Henry and turn his mind towards higher values represented by the mountains, which correspond to the delectable mountains of Bunyan's *The Pilgrim's Progress*. Like Christian of *The Pilgrim's Progress*, Henry starts at the 'City of Destruction', described in the opening chapter (where only six thousand troops die of cholera), and passes through the 'Slough of Despond' (wound and hospitalization), 'the Valley of Humiliation (the Caporetto retreat), 'the Valley of the Shadow of Death' (arrest and shooting by the Italian Battle Police) and close association with Faithful who dies in Vanity Fair (Catherine who dies in the hospital). Like Christian's journey, Henry's is a soul's progress on the narrow path keeping in view the twinkling light of love as defined by the priest until he (as soul) reaches the Celestial City, which is beyond our view and cannot be described. But like the Abruzzi, it remains the destination, which Henry is yet to reach.

Before the adventurous boat journey to Switzerland, Henry goes from Milan to Stresa, where he lodges in a hotel. Catherine joins him. They are happy together, never feeling alone or insecure. He is filled with love and admiration for Catherine, who without any hesitation or second thought throws in her lot with him, at a time when he is a fugitive from the Battle Police, and could be arrested and shot any moment if caught. Her action is governed by her love for him which does not admit any selfish consideration. She is prepared to follow him to the ends of the earth and face any kind of hazard together with him. Henry reflects on her bravery and strength of character thus:

> If people bring so much courage to this world, the world has to kill them to break them, so of course it kills them. The world breaks everyone and afterward many are strong at the broken places. But those that will not break it kills. It kills the very good and the very gentle and the very brave impartially. If you are none of these you can be sure it will kill you too but there will be no special hurry (193).

H.R. Stoneback considers this passage the most eloquent in the book besides being sound Catholic and Christian doctrine and, as such, the heart of Hemingway's vision. He quotes Scott Fitzgerald's view that this passage is wonderful. Stoneback makes the following comment on this passage: being sound Christian doctrine and, as such, the heart of Hemingway's vision. He quotes Scott Fitzgerald's view that this:

> ... Hemingway is writing from the heart of Christian tradition, that Christ knows and Dostoevsky knows and Hemingway knows that if we are to live truly within the dispensation of the radical insufficiency of the human condition, we must suffer to be redeemed, and, with

> healing grace, we can be very "strong at the broken places." It is a natural fact, a spiritual fact (65-66).

Central to the Christian tradition is suffering or sacrifice. It is the Cross that Jesus bore and the crown of thorns that he wore. The thorny path is the Christian's choice. Suffering is followed by redemption and grace. The sufferings of Jesus and the persecution of the early Christians have made Christianity the most widely practised religion. Jesus died on the Cross but he and his Cross have become powerful icons of the religion he preached and founded. Catherine dies in childbirth, but she will always be remembered for the kind of love she symbolizes. The inscrutable power that we call God showers His grace on those who suffer in his name or for a good cause or for any of his creatures. There are two more interesting passages referring to that power—one, in which it is called 'they' and the other in which we have to read between the lines, for it is only suggested but not stated. The former follows the information given to Henry that his child had died:

> I had no religion but I knew he ought to have been baptized. But what if he never breathed at all. He hadn't. He had never been alive. Except in Catherine. I'd felt him kick there often enough. But I hadn't for a week. Maybe he was choked all the time. Poor little kid. I wished the hell I'd been choked like that. No I didn't. Still there would not be all this dying to go through. Now Catherine would die. That was what you did. You died. You did not know what it was about. You never had time to learn. They threw you in and told you the rules and the first time they caught you off base they killed you (251-252).

Who are 'they'? Are they the Gods on Mount Olympus? Or are they the Fates? Or is it some unknown power? Whatever the name in religion or mythology, it means God. We in our ignorance of the divine dispensation, think that God is doing all this out of some incomprehensible malice or sadistic intentions. We judge God by our standards—human standards, little realizing that we cannot understand God, not to speak of judging Him. God's ways are inscrutable and we cannot understand them with our limited mental capabilities. He acts in mysterious ways which baffle us sometimes. As William Cowper puts it:

> God moves in a mysterious way
> His wonders to perform (*Olney Hymns,* 35).

This truth can be read between the lines in the following passage which is more or less a continuation of the one cited above. Henry has just learnt about the death of his child and knows that Catherine is struggling against death. He recalls an incident from the past when he put a log on top of the fire in camp. As the log started burning, the ants came out and went first towards the centre where the fire was and then turned back and moved towards the end. There was not enough room at the end and some of them fell into the fire:

> I remember thinking at the time that it was the end of the world and a splendid chance to be a Messiah and lift the log off the fire and throw it out where the ants could get off on to the ground. But I did not do anything but throw a tin cup of water on the log, so that I would have the cup empty to put whisky in before I added water to it. I think the cup of water on the burning log only steamed the ants (252).

This distant memory of a camp experience has interesting things to tell us—Henry, on seeing the ants on the log, felt like a Messiah and thought of saving the ants by lifting the log off the fire and throwing it out. But there was a communication gap between this Messiah and God, who created a confusion in the mind of Henry. As a result, Henry, instead of throwing the log off the fire, threw a tin cup of water on the log. He wanted to use the cup for whisky and emptied it on the log. This is an ironic gap which appears everywhere in the world to the discerning eye. We plan to do something and end up doing its opposite and thus, with the best of intentions, do the wrong thing.

If we are humble and trust in God, without entertaining foolish egotistical notions about ourselves, our mental antennae receive the right directions from God. The will of God will then be revealed to us. Henry assumes the role of a Messiah and saviour and ends up as a cruel destroyer. But all this had happened a long time before and Henry is a chastened man now, with a better understanding of God's mysterious ways. There is nothing for us to do except pray. Humility and surrender to the will of God hold the key to peace and sanity. We have to acknowledge the superior mind, will, and power of God who designs everything and who knows what to do with our souls. All we can do is pray. With this unstated realization expressed by the passage about the ants, Henry prays to God:

> I knew she was going to die and I prayed that she would not. Don't let her die. Oh, God, please don't let her die. I'll do anything for you if you won't let her die. Please, please, please don't let her die. God, please make her not die. I'll do anything you say if you don't let her die (254).

Henry knew that she was going to die and still prayed hoping against hope. He does not say that Catherine may die when he prays but says with certainty that she is going to die. His prayer is very earnest and expresses his love for Catherine. But his knowledge that she is going to die in spite of his prayer has certainty about it. As a believer, he now knows she will die and still prays.

He goes in and finds Catherine on her deathbed. She faces death bravely and continues to have the same convictions as before. When he offers to bring a priest for confession she turns down that offer:

> 'Do you want me to get a priest or anyone to come and see you?'
>
> 'Just you', she said. Then a little later, 'I'm not afraid. I just hate it' (254).

He thinks of a priest for her in her last moments but she thinks only of him. He believes in Christianity while she believes only in him ('Just you') reminding us of Milton's Adam and Eve:

> "He for God only, she for God in him" *(Paradise Lost*, IV, 147).

H.R. Stoneback analyses the ants-on-the-log passage thoroughly:

> What *does* the passage actually tell us? (1) in nature, random suffering and random deliverance seem to be the scheme of things; (2) we have no power over nature, which remains inscrutable, mysterious, and contingent; (3) if Frederic failed to save the ants, while deeming it the right thing to do, that is the mark of his humanity, his defective will; (4) Frederic is not the Messiah, nor are human beings merely ants; (5) the passage demonstrates not "nihilism" or "futility" but one of the most familiar notions of Judeo-Christian tradition, the inscrutability of providence.... (67).

It is significant that Henry remembers the log at a critical time. It is also significant that, in the recollected episode, he had planned to act the role of a Messiah for the ants. The fact of the matter is that the log played the role of a saviour for Henry at a very critical moment. When he escapes from the Carabinieri and jumps into the Tagliamento, with shots ringing behind him, a log of timber comes to his rescue in the water like a god-send:

> When I came up the second time I saw a piece of timber ahead of me and reached it and held on with one hand. I kept my head behind it and did not even look over it. I did not want to see the bank. There were shots when I ran and shots when I came up the first time. I heard them when I was almost above water. There were no shots now. The piece of timber swung in the current and I held it with one hand. I looked at the bank. It seemed to be going by very fast .... I held on to the timber with both hands and let it take me along. The shore was out of sight now (176).

The piece of timber figures three times in the above passage: first, when it appears as if sent by God, and he holds it with one hand and takes shelter behind it from the shots; second, when it takes him fast away from the bank; and third, when he holds it with both hands and drifts fast with it until the shore disappears. Thus the log of wood came as a Messiah and saved his life while he had pretended to be a Messiah and thought of saving the ants from the log on the fire but mistranslated that thought into wrong and harmful action by throwing a cup of water on the heated log. He had acted like a fake Messiah—an antichrist—while the log of wood acted like a true Messiah. This reveals the mysterious way in which God acts: He deflates the ego of a simple, well-meaning person, whose intentions are good but ego is inflated with the desire to play a Messiah. He turns a prospective benefactor into a destroyer. The ego is the villain in the camp episode. But, as Henry remembers it, he has the advantage of hindsight and the intervening time which gives him maturity of understanding and humility. Once humility comes to him, his vanity disappears and he is able to pray. Once he prays, his mind becomes tranquil and he has a better understanding of God's ways.

This explains Henry's calmness at the end of the novel. There is no doubt that he is very sad at his bereavement, but, after the initial shedding of tears by dying Catherine's bed-side, we find Henry gaining a rare tranquillity and equanimity. There is no bitterness in his attitude to the doctor or the hospital staff. Catherine's only request before her death is that Henry should not do their "things with another girl, or say the same things". She wants him to have girls. Later, she promises to stay with him in the nights and assures him that she is not afraid of death.

Henry waits outside in the hall patiently for a long time. When the nurse tells him that Catherine's condition is serious he calmly asks "Is she dead?" The nurse answers "No, but she is unconscious." Then he goes into the room and stays with Catherine until she dies after a series of haemorrhages. All this he does without losing his cool and self-possession. He politely declines the doctor's offer to take him back to the hotel. He sends the nurses out of the room and spends a moment in the room to say goodbye to Catherine: "It was like saying good-bye to a statue" (256). Then he walks back to the hotel. Henry is in full control of his faculties and manages to check his emotion in the hour of his greatest grief.

He says goodbye (God be with you) to Catherine like one who knows that death is not the end, for the soul is immortal.

When he was wounded and had a near-death experience, he knew that he was the immortal soul and it would be a mistake to think that you just died. What holds good for himself holds good for Catherine too, and this gives him an unruffled mind in the face of Catherine's death.

CATHERINE

We hear about Catherine for the first time in Chapter 3, when Rinaldi tells Henry that he is in love with Miss Barkley and will probably marry her. Then he asks Henry whether it would be right to do so.

Next day Rinaldi takes Henry to the British Hospital. They meet Catherine Barkley and Miss Ferguson in the garden. He talks with Catherine while Rinaldi talks with Miss Ferguson. Henry finds her tall, blonde and beautiful, with a tawny skin and grey eyes, and carrying a thin rattan stick like a toy riding crop, bound in leather. This stick is like a magic wand, which calls up the sad romantic past of Catherine.

Henry asks, "What is the stick?" and Catherine answers that it belonged to her lover who was killed in France the previous year. His mother sent it to her along with his other things. We also learn that they grew up together and were engaged for eight years. She is repentent that they did not marry and she wanted to cut off her beautiful hair after his death:

> I wanted to do something for him. You see I didn't care about the other things and he could have had it all. He could have had anything he wanted if I had known. I would have married him or anything. I know all about it now. But then he wanted to go to war and I didn't know (19).

She has a silly fancy that he might come to her hospital with a sabre-cut and a bandage around his head or a wound in his shoulder. But that did not happen and he was blown to pieces. Her romantic fancy was blown to bits in that way.

From the above it becomes clear that Catherine is given to a romantic cast of mind. She is sorry that she did not give herself to him before his death for that would have given both of them a sense of fulfilment. She says, "He could have had anything he wanted if I had known." All these show her as a highly strung, romantic, sentimental and selfless lover, whose nature is to give rather than take pleasure.

The next afternoon Henry meets Catherine again in the garden of the British Hospital. During their conversation, he puts his arm around her and tries to kiss her. Her reaction is sharp and fast—a stinging slap. For her it is a violation of her privacy which includes memories of her beloved boyfriend while for him it is like a game of chess in which he plans his next moves carefully. She relents a little later, thaws a little, apologizes, calls him sweet, and says:

> 'Yes. You are a dear. I'd be glad to kiss you if you don't mind.'
>
> I looked in her eyes and put my arm around her as I had before and kissed her. I kissed her hard and tried to open her lips; they were closed tight. I was still angry and as I held her suddenly she shivered. I held her close against me and could feel her heart beating and her lips opened and her head went back against my hand and then she was crying on my shoulder.
>
> 'Oh, darling', she said. 'You will be good to me, won't you?' (25).

The above passage makes it clear that Catherine is highly strung and passionate by nature. She allows him to kiss her on the mouth, cries on his shoulder and calls him 'darling' in the second meeting itself.

Henry meets her again after two days. The conversation which ensues confirms our perception of her character that once such a person falls in love, she goes to the extreme position and loves her man with all her heart and all her soul, even to the extent of effacing herself and surrendering her individuality to her lover. She is hypersensitive, highly imaginative and emotional, and somewhat intuitive into the bargain.

> She looked at me. 'And you do love me?'
> 'Yes.'
> 'You did say you loved me, didn't you?'
> 'Yes', I lied. 'I love you.' I had not said it before.
> 'And you call me Catherine?'
> 'Catherine....'

They walk for a while and stop under a tree, where they resume their conversation.

> 'Say, "I've come back to Catherine in the night".'
> 'I've come back to Catherine in the night.'
> 'Oh, darling, you have come back, haven't you?'
> 'Yes.'
> 'I love you so and it's been awful. You won't go away?'
> 'No, I'll always come back.'
> 'Oh, I love you so ....' I thought she was probably a little crazy. It was all right if she was. I did not care what I was getting into. This was better than going every evening to the house for officers where the girls climbed all over you ... I knew I did not love Catherine Barkley nor had any idea of loving her. This was a game like bridge, in which you said things instead of playing cards (27-28).

Catherine's intuitive mind catches Henry's hypocrisy. She probes his mind with her X-ray eye and discovers that he is playing a mean game and that he thinks she is crazy. She points out that he is playing a rotten game and gently admonishes him:

> 'You're a nice boy', she said. 'And you play it as well as you know how. But it's a rotten game.'
>
> 'Do you always know what people think?'
>
> 'Not always. But I do with you. You don't have to pretend you love me. That's over for the evening. Is there anything you'd like to talk about?'
>
> 'But I do love you.'
>
> 'Please let's not lie when we don't have to. I had a very fine little show and I'm all right now. You see I'm not mad and I'm not gone off. It's only a little sometimes' (28).

She calls Henry a nice boy even as she called her dead boyfriend “a very nice boy”. But her boyfriend was going to marry her while Henry is playing an uncharitable game with her which she describes as “rotten”. She knows that he is pretending to love her and tells him that his game is up and the little show is over for the evening. She collects herself controlling her emotions and declares that she is all right now and not mad unveiling his passing suspicion that she is crazy.

Thus we find that Catherine may be highly strung and emotional but she has the power to control herself and act in a strong, responsible way. She has an uncanny, intuitive perception and can see through the games of people and read their minds. In short, she is a strong, stable character who can take care of herself though she is capable of loving with all her heart and of giving herself to her lover without holding back anything. She is the archetypal female, the ultimate mother-figure. Henry wrote to his family before falling in love with Catherine, but, as she becomes an increasingly mothering presence to him, he sheds what little commitment he has to his family and stops writing to them. Hemingway who himself was androgynous, as pointed out by Kenneth Lynn, was nervous about mothering women, and projected this on to Henry, who considers total surrender to Catherine's femininity as engulfment. Catherine's femininity is a powerful force in *A Farewell to Arms.*

Catherine bears the name of Saint Catherine of Siena, who nursed the sick, and Saint Catherine of Alexandria, known for her great suffering, the former in particular, from the *Book of Saints*. Catherine Barkley, like Saint Catherine of Siena, is a nurse. Besides, Saint Catherine of Siena is the patron saint of Italy together with Saint Francis of Assisi. Catherine gives Henry a Saint Anthony medal as a protective talisman. Henry wears it around his neck. Later, after being wounded, he loses it, probably at one of the dressing stations, and forgets about it. Michael Reynolds, in his valuable book, *Hemingway's First War*: *The Making of A Farewell to Arms,* says that “the Saint Anthony medal for hopeless circumstances” was stolen from him at the dressing station (245). Reynolds notices ironic touches to the incident.

Saint Anthony is invoked for the return of lost property, for the protection of travellers. There is no reference anywhere to Saint Anthony as the patron of hopeless circumstances. Catherine has only a vague faith in Saint Anthony as a protective medal. Like all talismans, which derive their strength from the wearer's faith, Catherine's St. Anthony, which she has given away after wearing it for some time, performs his functions partially. Catherine loses and finds Henry. Henry, who may be treated as a traveller in Italy is protected. But Catherine's pregnancy is not protected. The medal itself shows St. Anthony holding a child, probably the child-Christ. Stoneback calls attention to the irony here: "The ironies reverberate, extensively and intensively, for Frederic's Saint Anthony, after he has performed one primary function, is himself 'lost' (not necessarily 'stolen' as Reynolds says) and thus unavailable to Catherine when she needs protection" (50).

Catherine is not made in the image of the highly individualistic, emancipated and self-willed Western woman. She puts us in mind of the Oriental woman, the Indian woman in particular, with extraordinary loyalty to her man. She is a bright example of the Hindu concept of *pativrata*, the docile woman totally dedicated to her husband who is her God. Such a woman lives for her husband only and she has no life of her own. Catherine, too, falls into this category of devoted lovers. In fact, this is not an Oriental concept only. This is the traditional Christian and Western concept also, beautifully described and glorified in Milton's *Paradise Lost*, when he describes Adam and Eve in the Garden of Eden: "He for God only, she for God in him" (IV, ll. 147). Later, during the course of their conversation, Eve speaks thus to Adam:

> 'My author and disposer, what thou bidd'st
> unargued I obey, so God ordains;
> God is thy law, thou mine; to know no more
> Is woman's happiest knowledge and her praise.
> With thee conversing I forget all time, ...' (483-487).

Compare this with Catherine's words in the hospital:

> 'I'll do what you want and say what you want ...
> I want what you want. There isn't any me any more. Just what you want' (84).

Even though Henry and Catherine feel like a married couple, the fact remains that they are not married. Henry is keen on marriage but Catherine does not want it as they are so deeply in love with each other that marriage is not necessary and also because of her fear that she will be sent away until the war is over. She does not want to leave him.

> '... What good would it do to marry now? We're really married. I couldn't be any more married.'
>
> 'I only wanted to for you.'
>
> 'There isn't any me. I'm you. Don't make up a separate me' (90).

There is a reference to religion as Henry proposes a private kind of marriage during the course of the same conversation when Catherine sounds like a Hindu *pativrata*, whose only religion is her husband:

> 'Couldn't we be married privately some way? Then if anything happened to me or if you had a child.'
>
> 'There is no way to be married except by church or state. We are married privately. You see, darling, it would mean everything to me if I had any religion. But I haven't any religion.'
>
> 'You gave me the Saint Anthony.'
>
> 'That was for luck. Someone gave it to me.'
>
> 'Then nothing worries you?'
>
> 'Only being sent away from you. You're my religion. You're all I've got' (91).

In the ancient Hindu society, there were four types of marriages: (1) *Brahma* or the traditional marriage in accordance with the rites laid down by scriptures, (2) *Gandharva* or the marriage of lovers, where only love mattered and no scriptural injunctions, (3) *Rakshasa* or the marriage of lovers who elope together or where the bridegroom carries away the bride who loves him, in the face of opposition from her family or community, and (4) *Paisachika* or a brutal kind of marriage in which the lover abducts the girl and marries her against her will.

The marriage Henry and Catherine enter into here is the *Gandharva* type. But there is neither religious nor social sanction for this kind of marriage in any country or society today even though it was widely accepted in ancient India. In some Western countries this kind of marriage is slowly being accepted here and there as a living-in relationship, but still the legal problems in regard to the offspring, inheritance and separation are not sorted out. Love and loyalty provide the basis for this kind of marriage.

Henry, being a religious minded person, is worried about the future of Catherine and her offspring in the event of anything happening to him. He is worried about their economic and social security. There are only two kinds of marriages available to them—the religious and the civil—which could ensure economic and social security to Catherine and her offspring and put the marriage in a legal frame. But such a marriage would separate them by taking Catherine, the nurse, away from Henry. When Catherine declares that she has no religion, Henry reminds her of the St. Anthony talisman, which she gave him. But she explains that she gave it for luck and not for any religious considerations. Since lack of religious faith generally causes anxieties, Henry asks her if nothing worries her; she answers that her only worry is being sent away from him and makes a firm declaration, "You're my religion. You're all I've got" like Milton's Eve or a good, loyal wife of the bygone times, or like the *pativrata* (one who worships her husband) of ancient India, for whom the husband is the only religion.

Catherine has a psychic side to her character which is explained by her highly emotional nature. She reads the thoughts of Henry in their first three meetings and sees through his play-acting as a lover. Thirteen chapters later, we find that she has a premonition of her death when she talks of her fear of the rain: "I'm afraid of the rain because sometimes I see me dead in it" (100).

She is brave and adventurous. These qualities which are manifest throughout the novel display themselves prominently when they row across the lake from Italy to Switzerland on a stormy night with the wind in their faces. The going is rough and the distance they cover is about thirty kilometers. They row all night in the wind and the rain. When his hands are sore, Catherine helps with the steering and the oar. He sits in the back and watches Catherine row like *Lord Krishna* watching his wife, *Satyabhama* fight with the demon-king, *Naraka*, while he rests. Henry has always admired Catherine's bravery and pays her this tribute in an oft-quoted passage of a philosophical reflection on the world and its brave children:

> If people bring so much courage to this world, the world has to kill them to break them, so of course it kills them. The world breaks everyone and afterward many are strong at the broken places. But those that will not break it kills. It kills the very good and the very gentle and the very brave impartially. If you are none of these you can be sure it will kill you too but there will be no special hurry (193).

This memorable passage is a powerful comment on the hostile world in which we live and how it throws challenges to the brave in order to humble them or break them and in the process it has to kill them. The passage points to Catherine's tribulations and the death awaiting her on the other shore of the lake, in Switzerland.

Once they cross the lake and feel safe at Montreux in the mountains of Switzerland, things move at breakneck speed as the biological trap closes in on Catherine. They are secure and safe from external dangers like the battle police but the internal dangers like labour pains, caesarian operation and haemorrhages lead to Catherine's death.

Catherine is not afraid of anything in life nor of life after death. When she is on her deathbed, Henry goes to her bedside. She feels sorry for him and tries to comfort him while, generally, it should be the other way round: "Poor darling. You touch me all you want" (254). When Henry offers to bring a priest, which is necessary for life after death, or anyone else, she says, "Just you... I'm not afraid. I just hate it" (254). Moments before her death we find this touching scene in which Catherine faces death bravely and promises to stay with Henry in the night even after death:

> 'All right', Catherine said. 'I'll come and stay with you in nights', she said. It was very hard for her to talk.
>
> 'Please go out of the room', the doctor said. Catherine winked at me, her face grey. 'I'll be right outside', I said.
>
> 'Don't worry, darling', Catherine said. 'I'm not a bit afraid. It's just a dirty trick.'
>
> 'You dear, brave sweet' (255).

Catherine is not at all afraid. She playfully winks at Henry and promises to join him in the nights even after death. She is truly a "dear, brave sweet" as he calls her.

In the end, Henry spends a moment alone with Catherine in the room. "It was like saying good-bye to a statue." Stoneback finds "the sacrament of adoration" here:

> It may not be "any good"—what would be?—for Frederic in his darkest moment, but isn't it better, more seemly and decorous, more intelligent, more Catholic, more trully loving, for Frederic to say "good-by"—i.e. "God be with you"—to a well-made, well-loved "statue", the spirit, the soul of which has gone elsewhere yet will somehow always be with him, than for Frederic to bid adieu to a cold corpse that must go into the ground? (71).

Thus, Catherine is like a monument on a pedestal after her death—a monument for love and loyalty in a woman and for exemplary femininity, with her soul yearning to spend the nights with her lover.

THE PRIEST

The priest is the 'code hero' in *A Farewell to Arms*, to use a term from the traditional Hemingway criticism. He is the code hero while Frederic Henry is the hero. The code hero is the *guru* figure who teaches the code to the hero—the mentor from whom the hero learns and by whom he is initiated. Earl Rovit calls him the 'tutor' for the hero who is called 'tyro'.

It is not without significance that the priest is the very first character portrayed in the novel, for *A Farewell to Arms* is, perhaps, the most religious of all Hemingway's novels. It has an abundance of spiritual and Catholic details, images and symbols. The composition of this novel coincides with the personal life of Hemingway soon after his conversion to the Catholic faith. Stoneback notes that in at least thirty-two of the forty-one chapters of the novel, there are religious references and allusions (49).

Henry sits with a friend drinking from a bottle of Asti and looking out at the snowfall outside through the "window of the bawdy-house, the house for officers."

> My friend saw the priest from our mess going by in the street, walking carefully in the slush, and pounded on the window to attract his attention. The priest looked up. He saw us and smiled. My friend motioned for him to come in. The priest shook his head and went on ....
>
> The priest was young and blushed easily and wore a uniform like the rest of us but with a cross in dark red velvet above the left breast-pocket of his grey tunic (9-10).

The priest is young and wears a uniform like the others but with a cross in dark red velvet above the left breast-pocket. He walks carefully in the slush and blushes and smiles easily. Henry sees the priest from the bawdy-house. His friend signals for him to come in but the priest refuses. Henry in the whore-house provides the foil for the priest who never enters it. Besides, Henry sitting in the whore-house represents carelessness about himself and his soul while the priest walking carefully in the slush represents the holy man moving carefully in the slush of the pleasures of the world. The blush and smile on his face speak of innocence and purity. Henry in the house of corruption aspires to the pure state of the priest.

Later, in the mess, the captain and others tease the priest. Henry tries to change the subject by referring to the weather and the forced cessation of fighting owing to snowfall. Then the major suggests that Henry should go on leave and relax in places like Rome, Naples or Sicily. The others suggest other places like Amalfi, Palermo and Capri. But the priest wants him to go to the Abruzzi and visit his family at Capracotta. Henry's other companions suggest worldly temptations but the priest points to the pure heights the soul should try to attain. The priest is a true well-wisher of Henry and exercises a healthy influence on him. The narrator gives the priest priority by presenting him before any other character in the novel—even Catherine. He tries to lift up Henry to the pure air of the Abruzzi and its virtues. He is to teach Henry about true, selfless love later. Henry forgets the teaching but realizes its value later. Since the narrative is retrospective and there is some considerable interval between the time of action and the time of narration, Henry refers to it early in his narration, in the third chapter, soon after his return from leave. He expresses his regret that he has not gone to the Abruzzi:

> ... he understood that I had really wanted to go to the Abruzzi but had not gone and we were still friends with many tastes alike, but with the difference between us. He had always known what I did not know and what, when I learned it, I was always able to forget. But I did not know that then, although I learned it later (15).

Reynolds cites the priest's teaching about love, sacrifice and service and says: "As Frederic admits, he is always able to forget those things which the priest knew" (252).

The importance of the Abruzzi lies not only in its being a "clear cold and dry" place with good hunting but in its being a country where "a man may love God. It is not a dirty joke" (60). This love of God may be what Henry learns later. Stoneback argues forcefully thus:

> It is not the primary business of the priest—the priest of *A Farewell to Arms* or any priest—to be matchmaker, guide to romantic love, interpreter of 'domestic values' or hunting guide, the priest is the shepherd of souls (42).

The priest's role as 'tutor' or the 'ideal figure' is central to the novel. According to Carlos Baker, the sacred-versus-profane-love-antithesis is quietly emphasized in the novel (108).

Earl Rovit comments thus on the effect of this antithesis on Henry:

> Rinaldi, as he later describes himself, is "the snake of reason", or the rationalization of not-caringness, the priest is his opposite number, the dove of faith, the consecration of *caritas* ... although Frederic will come to a balance somewhere between Rinaldi and the priest, the rest of the novel will be an uninterrupted progress away from Rinaldi (102).

Rovit takes the position that Henry strikes a balance between Rinaldi and the priest in the early portions but later moves away from Rinaldi towards the priest's philosophy of love and life.

The priest accepts the baiting graciously as a joke. The second chapter, in which the priest is introduced, introduces questions of faith, atheism and Freemasonry, in the book titled *Black Pig*, which cavils at faith, and the Abruzzi, the land of joy, purity and peace. The priest, with his smile of tolerance and understanding, dominates the chapter. The Abruzzi motif extends to the next chapter also. The priest is closely associated with the pure air of the mountains.

Later, Henry goes through the 'baptism of fire' at the front and gets experiential knowledge of the soul and its immortality in his near-death experience. What the priest has always stood for and taught, *viz.* the existence and imperishability of the soul is confirmed now for Henry. Soon after this we find Henry praying (48) and his legs are marked with 'a cross' (51) in the process of dressing his wound. Stoneback has this to say on this matter:

> Just as it was for Hemingway, who dated his conversion to Catholicism from the battlefield wound, this is for Frederic "the wound that made him think", as Hemingway described St. Ignatius Loyola's similar wound (at Pamplona) which made him think, which led to his conversion.... After the wounding, of course, Frederic's engagement with the true concerns of the priest, as shepherd of souls, deepens considerably (44).

The wound is not merely a physical thing here but a spiritual eye-opener. It brings Henry closer to the priest at the psychic level and prepares him for the teaching of the priest in Chapter 11.

In Chapter 10, Rinaldi visits Henry in the hospital and in Chapter 11, the priest. Rinaldi brings cognac and tells Henry that the priest is coming to see him. He talks vulgarly, insinuates that the priest and Henry are homosexuals, and suggests that Henry is really like himself (Rinaldi) underneath, playing the snake of *The Old Testament* and tempting Henry in a subtle way.

In the next chapter, the priest comes looking tired, but with the usual smile of understanding and tolerance on his face. He brings a mosquito net, a bottle of vermouth and some copies of *The News of the World.* During their conversation, the priest expresses his wish to live in the Abruzzi and love God and serve Him. When asked if he does not love God, Henry answers, "I am afraid of Him in the night sometimes" (Later on, in the novel, Henry tells Count Greffi that his devotion comes only at night):

> 'You should love Him.'
>
> 'I don't love much.'
>
> 'Yes', he said. 'You do. What you tell me about in the nights.'
>
> '*That is not love. That is only passion and lust, etc. When you love you wish to do things for. You wish to sacrifice for. You wish to serve*' (emphasis mine).
>
> 'I don't love'.
>
> 'You will. I know you will. Then you will be happy' (60).

Henry's statement that he is afraid of God reminds us of the Biblical words, "The fear of the Lord is the beginning of wisdom" (*Psalms,* CXI).

Stoneback holds the view that the priest seems to suggest that love of God and earthly love are inextricably bound up with each other:

> The priest is quite sure that Frederic will have this deep love and this knowledge will change him .... Frederic

> does finally have this other thing, first in his genuine love for Catherine and from that act of love, like ripples from a stone, a love that spreads and covers everything (45).

In fact, in the deeper layers of Henry's psyche, love is entrenched and he does not know that it is the love of God taking another manifestation as love for a woman. The priest, who is a spiritual psychiatrist, senses this, and helps in the birth of this love and its proper growth like a skilful obstetrician. He is a true educator ('educe' means 'draw out') and draws out the lover of God hiding in the depths of Henry's unconscious. The attractions of the flesh and senses keep this "love" buried under the debris of the waste of worldly joys and a spiritual *Guru* brings it out like an archaeological excavator. The human soul, initially, turns away and either hides itself or tries to escape somehow or other from the face of God, but God, like a loving parent, searches for the beloved soul and chases it if necessary before catching hold of it and holding it to His bosom, as described in Francis Thompson's *The Hound of Heaven*. Resistance to good and healthy things is very common like a patient's dislike of medicine and healthy food. The gap between what we really want and what we think we want has a role to play here. What we think we want is on the surface while what we really want is beneath the surface and hence out of sight. Henry really wants to go to the Abruzzi and its pure air and joys, but goes to cities like Rome, Naples and Milan to drown himself in pleasures. But the priest knows what he really wants. Henry realizes this later:

> He had always known what I did not know and what, when I learned it, I was always able to forget. But I did not know that then, although I learned it later (15).

When the priest visits wounded Henry in the field hospital, he asks the latter, "You do not want me for anything?" offering himself for either sacrament or confession or the Eucharist. Most probably, it is the Eucharist reserved for the sick and bedridden. Henry is not yet ready for it. After the priest leaves, Henry muses on the Abruzzi, the country of pure cold air, good hunting and good manners, where "it is understood that a man may love God".

The last two chapters, in which the priest appears (Chapters 25 and 26) show him and Henry closer than ever. In Chapter 25 they shake hands and the priest puts his hand on Henry's shoulder. Rinaldi teases the priest as before but the baiting does not affect him and he looks at Henry and smiles as if they shared a secret (135).

The priest repeats this in Chapter 26 before parting from Henry.

Rinaldi, in a drunken state, baits and mocks at the priest, who is gentle with him, though firm and untouched by the baiting. After Rinaldi and the major leave, Henry takes the priest to his room upstairs and the next chapter is devoted to their conversation. The talk is a subtle, engaging analysis of how people feel about the war. The priest feels that the war will be over soon as many people are gentle now and will stop fighting before long. Henry responds by saying that the Austrians, who have won victories will not stop fighting while the Italians, who are defeated may stop fighting like true Christians.

> '... It is in defeat that we become Christians.'
>
> 'The Austrians are Christians—except for the Bosnians.'
>
> 'I don't mean technically Christian. I mean like Our Lord.'
>
> He said nothing.
>
> 'We are all gentler now because we are beaten. How would Our Lord have been if Peter had rescued him in the Garden?'
>
> 'He would have been just the same.'
>
> 'I don't think so', I said (139).

It is clear that Henry talks like a well-versed Catholic here. The influence of the priest has worked quietly on Henry. We find Henry is moving in the direction intended for him by the priest, particularly when he glorifies defeat unconsciously ("It is in defeat that we become Christians"). Such a defeat born in the acceptance of the Lord's will is a victorious defeat. Stoneback points out that the priest is Henry's exemplar or tutor and shares with other Hemingway tutors "care, precision, good manners, proper appreciation of ritual, taste, ceremony, friendship, loyalty, and—above all—the sense of a shared secret knowledge (49).

COUNT GREFFI

> Count Greffi was ninety-four years old. He had been a contemporary of Matternich, and was an old man with white hair and moustache and beautiful manners. He had been in the diplomatic service of both Austria and Italy and his birthday parties were the great social events of Milan. He was living to be one hundred years old and played a smoothly fluent game of billiards that contrasted with his own ninety-four-year-old brittleness (196).

This is how Henry, the narrator, introduces Count Greffi to us. There is something in him that makes us think of the priest, particularly when he calls love a religious feeling. They play billiards and discuss the soul and religion while drinking wine. He refers to a book called *Mr. Britling Sees Through It.* Henry gives it a funny twist and says that he (H.G. Wells or Mr. Britling) does not see through it. The book was a best-seller in 1916. Henry sees the significance and humour in the combination of 'Brit' and 'ling'—'Brit' stands for the British, who are predominantly secularist and protestant and see very little.

When the Count remarks that the book is a good study of the English middle-class soul, Henry answers that he does not know about the soul. Count Greffi does not use the word 'soul' in the spiritual sense while Henry uses it in that sense. They use the same word in different senses—the secular and the spiritual. The Count who understands that Henry has used the word, 'soul', in the spiritual sense, asks him if he is *croyant* or devout. Henry answers that he gets his devotion only at night. He expresses the problems of the night when things are different. In *The Sun Also Rises* also Jake talks about how everything is different at night. When one is alone with oneself and experiences the fear of the unknown, one thinks of God and prays for help. In distress God comes to mind. This prompts the Count to make the confession, "I had expected to become more devout as I grow older but somehow I haven't" (202). He sounds sad. This remark gives us the feeling that the Count's soul is in the same stage of progress as Henry's when he says that the priest knows what he (Henry) really wants but does not know it. Count Greffi has a similar problem at ninety-four. He has always wanted to be more devout but forgets about it in his diplomatic activities, parties and billiards like Henry really wanting to go to the Abruzzi but going to the cities for sinful pleasures.

Then the conversation turns to the Count's age and body, spirit and wisdom. When Henry calls him wise, the Count says that the wisdom of old people is a fallacy and old people grow only careful but not wise. The Count asks Henry to pray for him if he ever becomes devout:

> 'And if you ever become devout pray for me if I am dead. I am asking several of my friends to do that. I had expected to become devout myself but it has not come.' I thought he smiled sadly but I could not tell. He was so old and his face was very wrinkled, so that a smile used so many lines that all gradations were lost (203).

The Count seems to be worried and unhappy about devotion not coming to him for he repeats the same statement again and again. He is so worried that he requests Henry to pray for him as if he had an apprehension that his own prayers, if he is able to pray, may not reach the Lord's ears, and if they do, may not be accepted by Him. When Henry promises to pray for him, he says reiterating his anxiety for a third time, "I had always expected to become devout. All my family died very devout. But somehow it does not come" (203).

He is afraid that he has outlived his religious feeling having lived so long. Henry responds to this by saying that his own religious feeling comes only at night. This is also a repetition of his earlier statement in answer to the Count's question "Are you *croyant*?"

When Henry says that his own religious feeling comes only at night, the Count makes a very significant statement: "Then you too are in love. Do not forget that is a religious feeling" (203). Like the priest Count Greffi believes that love is a religious feeling since love is God. We have already noted that the priest and the Count share certain convictions. If the priest is asked how love is a religious feeling, he would explain it thus: "When you love you wish to do things for. You wish to sacrifice for. You wish to serve." If the wish to do things for others, if the wish to sacrifice for others, and if the wish to serve others is not a religious feeling, one wonders what is. True religion is based on service and sacrifice; true love is also based on service and sacrifice; and, therefore, true love and true religion are one and the same. The priest and the Count share this conviction. They also share a feeling of loving kindness for Frederic Henry.

RINALDI

Rinaldi appears as a friend of wounded Nick in Chapter VI of *In our Time*. Nick, the early *avatar* of the Hemingway hero, who is wounded in the spine, sits against the wall of the church and tells his friend, Rinaldi, "Senta Rinaldo; Senta. You and me we've made a separate peace .... We're not patriots." The machine-gun fire in the street provides the background. The twisted bedstead and the damaged house symbolize a ruined love and a ruined home. Rinaldi is split into Rinaldi and Catherine Barkley in the novel. In the novel it is Rinaldi who introduces Henry to Catherine. In "A Very Short Story", the Red-Cross nurse, Luz, ditches her young lover, unlike Catherine who loves Henry with an exemplary devotion. The major, whom Luz expects to marry does not answer her letters and is reported to have contracted gonorrhoea later while in *A Farewell to Arms*, Rinaldi fears that he has syphilis.

In *A Farewell to Arms,* Rinaldi is throughout a good friend of Henry, full of banter and garrulity like Mercutio in *Romeo and Juliet,* lively but irreligious, making fun of the priest and calling himself "the snake of reason". Like Mercutio's role ending in the Third Act, Rinaldi's role ends in Chapter 25 in a novel of 41 chapters.

His character counterbalances that of the priest. He is a good looking young man from Amalfi and of Henry's age. He shares the room with Henry. He is a surgeon, a healer of human bodies, while the priest is a healer of human souls.

When he is introduced in the second chapter it is as the lieutenant baiting the priest along with the captain and the major. The priest advises Henry to spend his leave in the Abruzzi and Rinaldi asks him to go to Amalfi. Both write to their families asking them to look after Henry well. Henry maintains a delicate balance between the two and goes neither to the Abruzzi nor to Amalfi.

Unlike the priest, for whom love is a religious feeling, he takes love very lightly boasting to Henry, who has just returned from his leave, that he is in love with Miss Barkley and may marry her. Later, when he and Henry go to the British hospital he pays more attention to Miss Ferguson and leaves Henry in the company of Catherine.

Afterwards, while walking home, Rinaldi casually remarks, "Miss Barkley prefers you to me. That is very clear. But the little Scottish one is very nice. When asked if he likes her (Miss Ferguson) he says "no". This shows that his love is only skin deep and his attitude to it is playful.

The vignette in Chapter VI ends with the sentence, "Rinaldi was a disappointing audience." The friendship of Henry and Rinaldi is a mutually disappointing relationship, for Henry moves away from the "snake of reason" towards the angel of faith as the novel progresses.

Rinaldi serves as a foil for the priest. They always appear together—the priest as God's angel and Rinaldi as a messenger of the Devil—and sometimes Rinaldi comes first with his ribald talk which is countered by the seasoned soothing talk of the priest, who follows him.

There is a rare vivacity about Rinaldi. He comes to the bed of Henry like some whirlwind, kisses him and presents him with a bottle of cognac. He talks happily about his work as a surgeon. He gives Henry the news that he (Henry) is getting the silver medal for bravery. He also tells him in advance that the priest is coming to see him. Then he makes a mischievous insinuation, sounding like the Devil's agent, that the priest and Henry have a homosexual relationship.

> ' ... Sometimes I think you and he are a little that way, You know.'
>
> 'No, you don't.'
>
> 'Yes, I do sometimes. A little that way like the number of the first regiment of the Brigata Ancona.'
>
> 'Oh, go to hell.'
>
> He stood up and put on his gloves.
>
> 'Oh, I love to tease you, baby. With your priest and your English girl, and really you are just like me underneath.'
>
> 'No, I'm not.'
>
> 'Yes, we are. You are really an Italian. All fire and smoke and nothing inside....' (56).

The suggestion of an abnormal sexual relationship reveals a mindset which is associated with sin and the biblical story of Sodom and Gomorrha, which is strengthened by his reference to 'fire and smoke', which sounds like 'fire and brimstone'. He cavils at priests and religion and praises a sacrilegious book like *Black Pig* and calls himself, 'the snake of reason'.

But, all said and done, he is a lively person, a good surgeon and a great friend of Henry's who fades away from his life after Catherine's entry into it.

In this world of binaries, where the holy person is known by the existence of the unholy person, Rinaldi helps us appreciate the priest. Rinaldi is the high priest of sensual enjoyment while the priest is the high priest of 'pure love'. Rinaldi's vulgar reference, in Chapter 10, to the difference between a good girl and a woman, with a sly dig at Catherine reveals that his perceptions do not go beyond the flesh:

> ... I tell you something about your good women. Your goddesses. There is only one difference between taking a

> girl who has always been good and a woman. With a girl it is painful. That's all I know.' He slapped the bed with his glove. 'And you never know if the girl will really like it' (56).

Later, in Chapter 25, he tells Henry that married couples, who love each other do not like him as he is 'the snake'—'the snake of reason'—an allusion to the Biblical 'snake'.

It is interesting and significant that Rinaldi and the priest are presented together in the same chapter or in contiguous chapters. Thus, if Rinaldi meets Henry in Chapter 10, the priest meets him in Chapter 11, and when Rinaldi meets Henry in Chapter 25, the priest meets him in the same chapter but stays on into Chapter 26 also. As Chapter 27 opens, we find that Rinaldi is still asleep when Henry leaves, and we do not see him afterwards.

10

First Thoughts and Second Thoughts: Some Revisions in the First Draft

It was Hemingway's practice to prepare a list of possible titles and choose the best of them at the time of publishing his writing. The following titles were considered for *A Farewell to Arms* before the title was finally chosen according to Bernard Oldsey and Michael Reynolds:

1. Patriot's Progress
2. The World's Room
3. Death Once Dead
4. A Farewell to Arms
5. The Sentimental Education of Frederic Henry
6. Every Night and All
7. Nights and Forever
8. The Hill of Heaven

A Farewell to Arms has a story somewhat similar to that of *The Pilgrim's Progress*, as we have already seen in our discussion of Frederic Henry's character, but "The Pilgrim's Progress" is a better title than 'Patriot's Progress" for this story and, therefore, the weak title was discarded.

"The World's Room" comes from the famous ballad, "Edward", which has many versions including the Percy's *Reliques* version entitled "Edward, Edward" in *The Oxford Book of Ballads* and cited by Oldsey and Reynolds. In most versions of the ballad, Edward has killed his brother for some reason and expiates for his evil deed by sailing in an open boat, which was the common medieval punishment for fratricide in the world of the ballads. Except for Frederic's journey by an open boat on Lake Maggiore and his blistered hand and his words, "no hole in my side", which call up the image of Jesus on the Cross, there is no similarity between the story of the ballad and the story of the novel; but the concept of expiation which is central to Catholicism and the narrative itself, which is a long confession, might have suggested this title to Hemingway. But Hemingway, obviously, was not satisfied with this title as Henry is not guilty of any sin of the scale of fratricide for, most of the time in the story, he is at the receiving end—a victim and sufferer.

"The Hill of Heaven" is another title inspired by the ballad, "The Daemon-Lover". Except for the allusions to the "banks O'Italie" and the hills of heaven and hell, the ballad has no resemblance to the story of the novel.

"Every Night and All" was inspired by the ballad, "A Lyke—Wake Dirge". The first stanza as well as the last is:

> This ae nighte, this ae nighte,
> Every nighte and alle,
> Fire and fleet and candle-light,
> And Christe receive thy saule.

The prayer here expresses Frederic's anxiety regarding Catherine's soul as she has declared that she has no religion. The novel is a "dirge" for her. "Nights and Forever" appears to be his own variation on the "Every nighte and alle", which refers to Frederic's anxiety or fear of God or devotion at night. Hemingway must have found both these titles weak and rejected them.

"The Sentimental Education of Frederic Henry" seems to have been inspired by Flaubert's *L'Education Sentimentale* and a more recent classic, *The Education of Henry Adams*.

"Death Once Dead" comes from Shakespeare's Sonnet—146, ("And Death once dead, there's no more dying then") and refers to the condition of the soul like the other discarded titles.

"A Farewell to Arms", which seems to have appealed to Hemingway most, was supplied by George Peele's "Sonnet *ad finem*: A Farewell to Arms" (from *Polyhymnia*). Stoneback's comments on how and why this poem struck the fancy of Hemingway as the aptest possible title for the novel are illuminating:

> In Peele's poem the former warrior, the ex-knight, prays to be allowed toward the end ("ad finem") to become a "beadsman", to turn his "lovers' sonnets" into "holy psalms" (Count Greffi, too, had expected to "become devout" toward the end). Oldsey, who in part illuminates and in part obfuscates what he recognizes as the rich "allusive force" of the Peele poem and the way that Hemingway's novel incorporates its motifs, construes... the main thrust to be the change of the knight/soldier into "wordsman" (29-34). This is to miss... the property of the poem and the novel which is expressed by Frederic's statement that he "might become very devout." For he is both "wordsman" and "beadsman" at once, in the act of telling the story which is simultaneously a lover's sonnet and a holy psalm (65).

Hemingway writes in the first draft of the manuscript: "And he smiled back." On second thoughts he adds "across the candle light" to the sentence. When we read "... and he smiled back across the candle light" (64/1, page 10), the priest's smile comes into relief. The priest is associated with light and health and the good things of life in the novel. His smile is the clean well-lighted place—a clean well-lighted smile. The priest- baiting takes place in the night, but the priest, the tyro or the *guru* figure, whose philosophy of love is central to the novel and lights it up, smiles across the candlelight.

A good example of how the writing gains by elimination of certain passages is provided by the removal of the quotations from Marvell in the first draft:

> '... and always at my back I hear
> Time's winged chariot hurrying near', I said.
> 'No, not that poem.'

'Thy beauty shall no more be found
Nor in thy marble panel shall sound
my echoing song.'
'No', said Catherine. 'No, it's not true.'
'The grave's a fine and private place
But none I think do there embrace.'
'I know that poem' Catherine said (64/6).

Only the first quotation is really relevant here and is retained on second thoughts and the scene becomes effective from the revision.

Sometimes, Hemingway's second thoughts caused him to remove certain passages but his second thoughts on these second thoughts counseled him not to remove them, e.g., the long beautiful passage in the middle of the Caporetto retreat beginning with "A retreat was no place for two virgins...." (153-154). Hemingway wrote in the margin of the first draft, "cut out maybe", but on second thoughts, retained it (64/8). This passage is analyzed by Charles R. Anderson in his illuminating essay "Hemingway's Other Style" anthologized by Carlos Baker in his *Ernest Hemingway*: *Critiques of Four Major Novels*, to which reference has already been made in the chapter on "Hemingway's Style". This remarkable passage would have been lost to posterity if Hemingway had not had second thoughts on his second thoughts.

Thus, a close study of the revisions reveals how the writing gains by adding a word or a phrase or a passage and, sometimes, by eliminating them.

The closing passage of the first draft of the novel is rejected by Hemingway. Here the narrator tells us in six foolscap pages that he could tell us what happened to the other characters, e.g., how Ettore became a fascist, how the priest lived in Fascist Italy, and how Rinaldi was cured of his syphilis, but first of all the business of the undertaker since Catherine was lying dead and so on (64/13). Hemingway discarded all that stuff and rewrote the conclusion in just twenty-nine short sentences, almost all of them declarative, and we have one of the finest conclusions in American fiction.

11

A Farewell to Arms as a Movie

Hemingway never liked the movie adaptations of his novels and stories and generally avoided the previews. The movie-makers are not always faithful to the text. Their criteria and motivations are different from the writers'. Their main interest is in the box-office. It is a world of big money where art is sacrificed for money. But a writer needs money like anybody else and if he tastes the joys money can buy when he is able to sell his writing, he will hunger for more money and more pleasures.

Hemingway is reported to have said:

> The best way for a writer to deal with Hollywood was to arrange a rendezvous with the movie men at the California state line. You throw your book, they throw you the money, then you jump into your car and drive like hell the way you came (Phillips, 6).

Most of the Hemingway movies make the readers and admirers of Hemingway unhappy. Hollywood has failed to find visual equivalents for his remarkable prose (Oliver, 33). According to Linda Dittmar, "Hemingway's work is not literally filmable under any circumstances. It can accommodate an audio-visual tribute but not literal translation" (Oliver, 58). He generally disapproved of the film versions of his novels and steadfastly refused to work on the screenplays of his fiction because he felt "as though you were looking through a camera lens. All you think about is pictures, when you ought to be thinking about people" (Beja, 27).

The appeal of Hemingway's prose is magical like Charles Dickens's prose that inspired Griffith's cinematographic innovations in his time. But Hemingway belonged to a group of writers who could never agree that their stories required expansion, modification and compression for adaptation to the screen. Some other members of this celebrated group were Virginia Woolf, Vachel Lindsay or Hannah Arendt, who have felt that the attempt of movie-makers to turn literature into a commercial visual commodity for mass consumption is synonymous with betrayal (Boyum, 6).

The question generally raised in this context is whether the film version is faithful to the text or not and, if it is faithful, how faithful, and if the spirit of the text is respected in the film. There are bound to be differences between the text of the novel/story and the screen version. The remarks of David Selznick, the MGM producer-director of "A Farewell to Arms" on this subject are interesting. In his letter to Robert Chapman (7 November 1956), he writes as follows:

> ... Hemingway is not easy to adapt as one might think ... Just pulling scenes out of Hemingway and putting them together results in a script that is not only unplayable and undramatizable but just doesn't even tell the story Hemingway tells. Hecht and myself went mad telling ourselves that Hemingway had this or that scene, only to find that it was not there at all! At least in words, but was somehow created by Hemingway's fantastic gift for giving the impression of a scene without actually writing it. As Hecht put it, 'that SOB writes in water!' (Behlmer, 443).

There are two movie versions of *A Farewell to Arms*. The first version was produced by Paramount Pictures and directed by Frank Burzage in 1932. It was a black-and-white movie in which Gary Cooper played the role of Frederic Henry and Helen Hays that of Catherine. Ben Glazer wrote the screenplay and Charles Lang was the cinematographer.

The first shot of this 1932 version focuses on a wounded soldier on a winding road. The camera then moves up and shows the river, the plain, and the mountains, in a long shot, and returns to the wounded soldier being picked up by an ambulance. As the vehicle moves away, Gary Cooper's (Henry's) voice is heard, "The man here is bleeding to death", and the driver's reply, "can't stop here, not now".

This episode occurs towards the end of the scene showing Frederic Henry in the army camp, in conversation with Rinaldi, the captain, the priest and others, with whom the novel proper commences in the second chapter, and is presented in a flashback. There is a remarkable sequence showing Henry being taken in a wheel chair into the hospital ward. The faces of nurses bending over are shown in a close shot from below. Finally Helen Hays enters the ward and bends down to kiss the wounded soldier.

The 1957 film version was made in colour with Rock Hudson and Jennifer Jones in the lead roles. It was a joint production of David O. Selznick and Twentieth Century Fox. The film credits Charles Vidor as the director. In fact, Vidor came into the movie when it was already partly made as his predecessor, John Huston, had left owing to his disagreement with Selznick over the screenplay done jointly by Ben Hecht and Selznick.

This movie opens with a close-up of a bell tolling over a large building. The camera moves over the beautiful landscape of mountains and valleys. The grazing cattle symbolize the basics of life, like feeding, loving and rearing children, which go on perennially in spite of wars, natural calamities and epidemics. Written words introduce the movie as a tragic love story of an American boy and an English girl in war-torn Italy—love in the time of war. Broken houses speak eloquently about the devastation caused by war. Soldiers march across the frame and the camera follows a tall man walking down the lane towards a building.

In both the movie versions, the novel is presented as a tragic love story. Borzage, whose "war" film, *No Greater Glory*, based on Molnar's historical play of 1907, became a great hit, gives *A Farewell to Arms* in 1932 and *History is*

Made at Midnight in 1935 similar romantic treatment. Selznick whose "Gone with the Wind" and "Rebecca" won him Academy Awards presents *A Farewell to Arms* as a wartime romance. Both cut down to the minimum scenes of war and focus on the emotional struggle of the hero rejecting war in favour or love and peace, creating a separate world of love and peace reminding us of the contemporary slogan, "Let us make love, not war". This is vividly presented by the Christmas-Card settings in the 1957 film. This film (1957) adheres more closely to the novel than the earlier one of 1932. It is also able to present more effectively Hemingway's philosophy of Nature and Time and his style of allusions and repetitions through the symbolic devices of bell, clock, rain, thunder and landscape. Maybe the contemporary mores of the time necessitated the marriage of the lovers in Borzage's film.

So far as the endings are concerned, the 1957 version is faithful to the text while the 1932 version makes a change for romantic effect. In the 1932 version, Henry carries dead Catherine to the open window and murmurs, "Peace, peace!" Bells ring, doves fly, and the music of 'Leibstod' from *Tristan and Isolde* fills the air. In the 1957 version, Frederic Henry walks slowly down a rain-drenched avenue to the accompaniment of 'Leibstod'. In both the versions, death is presented as an ascent or an avenue leading to spiritual transcendence.

Linda Dittmar makes the following observations on the employment of song and music in scenes of devastation:

> As we see a military convoy winding its way along a narrow mountain road, the recording apparatus singles out for us a lone harmonica's plaintive song, and while the camera regally pans across and up the mountainous expanse, a chorus of male voices resonates across this panorama. Sometime later, when the staff evacuates the military hospital, leaving the patients to die under the priest's spiritual if not medical protection, we hear the wounded burst forth in a marvelous rendition of *Ave Maria* as flames artistically frame the shot at its foreground (123).

The Ave Maria reference invokes purgatory and the prayer for redemption.

Hemingway's stories often seem to have been written for the screen. His plots, characters, and action seem famously adaptable to the screen. So are his safaris, bull-fights, and wars. His protagonists relate easily to the action heroes of Hollywood like Gregory Peck, Humphrey Bogart, William Holden and John Wayne.

But the challenge comes from the iceberg of his style with its expressed and suppressed or suggested meanings and the well-honed staccato sentences marching like the troops in *A Farewell to Arms*.

12

The Reception of *A Farewell to Arms*

Hemingway was a little worried about how *A Farewell to Arms* would fare, when it was published in 1929, as another novel about the great war, Erich Maria Remarque's *All Quiet on the Western Front* was also published the same year. It described the war from a German soldier's point of view and, translated into English, it became an immediate success and was made into a movie. Hemingway's novel was published later in 1929. It became a bestseller too and was made into a successful movie.

Hemingway, being a realistic writer, did not want to romanticize the rougher aspects of life. Since the subject included army life, his descriptions and dialogues were couched, sometimes, in vulgar but realistic language, the way people really speak. When he received the proofs, he found himself engaged in a friendly dispute with his editor, Max Perkins on this subject. Even after reluctantly pruning or concealing with blanks the objectionable words and phrases, the novel was criticized by some readers for its frankness and vulgar expressions, which were considered objectionable and offensive at that time. The serialized version in *Scribner's Magazine* was banned in Boston by the Superintendent of Police. The projected sale to the Literary Guild or the Book-of-the-Month Club was given up. The author and the publisher had to remove or change the objectionable words like *balls, fuck,* and *shit*.

When the book was published in September 1929, there was a flood of positive reviews. There were two negative reviews, but one of the reviewers, Harry Hansen of the *New*

York World, later changed his opinion. Another reviewer, Robert Herrick, wrote in *Bookman* under the title "What is Dirt?" and proceeded to answer the question, '*A Farewell to Arms*', and described it in very harsh words: "Unpleasant garbage." He also admitted condescendingly that he had read only half of the novel and that was enough for him to arrive at this conclusion.

A very influential critic by name, Henry Seidel Canby, wrote in the prestigious *Saturday Review of Literature* that the novel was "an erotic story, shocking to the cold, disturbing to the conventional who do not like to see mere impersonal amorousness lifted into a deep, fierce love involving the best in both man and woman .... As for Hemingway's frankness of language, to object to it would be priggish" (October 12, 1929).

Favourable reviews by other distinguished critics like Malcolm Cowley and Clifton Fadiman appeared. They both felt that Hemingway had written his best book surpassing himself. Cowley found the style "subtler and richer prose" appropriate to a changed attitude in which "emotions are more coloured by thought..." (*New York Herald Tribune*, October 6, 1929). Fadiman called it "a remarkably beautiful book. The very apotheosis of a kind of modernism" (*The Nation*, October 30, 1929).

Readers' tastes and cultural mores, and their views of what is right and what is wrong change with times. So does their use of language. As the language of literature has changed and the readers' views of words and phrases, which were considered offensive in the past, have also changed, other elements in fiction like the characters appear in a different light to readers with the changing times.

An important change in critical perception is with regard to the character of Catherine Barkley. Some of the early critical responses to the portrayal of Catherine were that it was one of the best features of the novel. *Boston Transcript* described her character "a very fine portrayal of a woman who was not afraid" (October 19, 1929). Others compared her with Lady

Brett Ashley, the tough heroine of *The Sun Also Rises* and found her love of the hero, Frederic Henry, bordering on a crazy devotion incredible, and commented that she was a man's dream-girl, little more than a far-fetched, romantic paste-board figure. Most of the early critics who thought that most of Hemingway's women characters were either male-destroying bitches or characterless dream-girls. In the early days of the feminist movement of the 1970s, Hemingway seemed to many feminist critics as the macho-male whose women, in life as well as in writing, were either housekeepers, cooks, and button-sewers, or sexual objects, but never thinking and feeling individuals in their own right. This feminist reaction to him was aggravated further by the popular macho-image of him, which appeared on the cover pages of the mass-circulation magazines like *Time* and *Life*. He was often seen in hunting, boxing, fishing, bull-fighting, and soldiering scenes. But Hemingway, the votary of art and serious literature, who was a committed writer, remained in the background.

Stimulated by the feminist movement and mainly by Judith Fetterley's book, *The Resisting Reader: A Feminist Approach to American Fiction*, Hemingway's work was re-examined in the light of the new perspectives. Fetterley focused attention on Catherine Barkley and in the following decade several books and essays were written on Hemingway's women characters. The posthumous publication of *The Garden of Eden* (1986) revealed his interest in androgyny and his ability to depict complex male-female relations. Comparisons were made between Catherine Barkley on one side, and Catherine Bourne and Marita on the other.

Another debate is on how Hemingway managed the dual themes of love and war—whether it is a war novel with a love story as part of it or a story of love in the time of war. If it is a predominantly war novel, the disappearance of war from the last section of the novel needs to be explained satisfactorily. If it is a love story, the emphasis on the hero's experiences as a soldier and a fugitive needs justification.

Hemingway's friend and fellow novelist, John Dos Passos, reviewed *A Farewell to Arms* in *New Masses*, a socialist journal. He praised the writer's craftsmanship and focused on the political context of the novel (December 1, 1929). The novel takes on a new dimension when studied from the point of view of the war as a class struggle, not of the Germans and Austrians versus the Italians and their allies, but of the *haves* versus the *have nots* in terms of power, money and distinction.

Donald Davidson, writing in *Nashville Tennessean*, studied the novel in the light of behavioural psychology, observing how the characters respond to external stimuli like laboratory animals. They are colourless and without souls (November 3, 1929). Wyndham Lewis levels the charge of anti-intellectualism against Hemingway in his essay "The Dumb Ox: A Study of Ernest Hemingway", in which he praised his style but criticized what he called his primitivism and his total rejection of the life of the mind.

Readers and critics approach works of literature with different tastes, experiences and expectations. The rich range of response to *A Farewell to Arms* speaks of the range and depth of the novel. Approached from New Critical (E.M. Halliday's study of symbolism and irony), Feminist, Marxist, Psychological, Religious and Historical angles, the novel grows in our minds. The novel has proved itself an excellent example of Hemingway's craftsmanship through the critical readings it has been subjected to for more than half a century.

Conclusion

We have studied *A Farewell to Arms* in the light of Hemingway's aesthetic principles and major themes. People have studied it for more than half a century as a great war novel and a great story of love. Since the drums of war retreat after the Caporetto retreat and fade away after Henry plunges into the Tagliamento and bids farewell to arms, the novel looks more like a story of love in the time of war.

> You were out of it now. You had no more obligation. If they shot floor-walkers after a fire in the department store because they spoke with an accent they had always had, then certainly the floor-walkers would not be expected to return when the store opened again for business. They might seek other employment; if there was any other employment and the police did not get them (181).

Henry is out of it (war). What remains is his love for Catherine. Thus, in the novel, the love-story outlives the war-story. But that does not mean the end of all problems. A story may have a happy ending but there is no happy ending in life. "They lived happily ever after" is an unrealistic conclusion, for death may come in any form, not necessarily as the explosion of a trench mortar or a gunshot. It may come as one of the hazards of childbirth, as it happens to Catherine. Poor Henry bids farewell to the arms of war and rushes to the arms of his beloved but soon finds himself bidding farewell to those arms also. In the end he is his lonely self like in the beginning—a philosophical thought, which makes us hark back to the concept of the soul or self. When we look at the novel as the story of the growth of Henry's soul, an amazing meaning is revealed through war and love. If the love-story outlives the war-story, the story of the soul outlives the love-story.

When we look at the story of the growth of Henry's soul, the priest and Catherine on one side and Rinaldi on the other assume considerable significance. Rinaldi, the snake of reason, fades away from Henry's life along with the arms of war, yielding place to Catherine and her arms of love. There is still the element of carnal love, but the purer love preached by the priest becomes stronger and stronger in his mind. The priest's words assume a central significance in the novel: "When you love you wish to do things for. You wish to sacrifice for. You wish to serve." In short, true love demands the effacement of self and all selfishness, which means only giving and no grabbing. Count Greffi endorses this when he describes love as a religious feeling. Thus Catherine becomes an icon for Henry's realization of love.

Catherine herself, in her own right, is the high priestess of the kind of love preached by the priest. She practises that love. Her love for Henry is absolutely unselfish. She gives without expecting anything for herself. She is not bothered about security for herself or for the child in her womb. Even when Henry offers marriage to ensure social and economic security for her and the child, she rejects it outright for that may cause their separation and she has complete faith in Henry besides. "There isn't any me. I'm you", and again "You're my religion. You're all I've got" (90, 91). She declares that she has no desires of her own, not even an existence of her own: "I want what you want. There isn't any me anymore. Just what you want" (84). Such a love may be in accordance with the priest's definition, but it sounds so unreasonable in the modern world, where there is equality of the sexes and where every person, male or female, has his or her own individuality. This merger of one's individuality in another's in the name of love is an old world ideal and is scoffed at and scorned today. But it cannot be denied that love, at a higher level, involves sacrifice and service, and an erasure of the ego and selfish considerations.

As a conscious craftsman, Hemingway uses suggestion and symbolism in a skilful way, sometimes, without appearing to do so. This is in accordance with his famous theory of the iceberg: "The dignity of movement of an iceberg is due to only one-eighth of it being above water" (*Death in the Afternoon*, 183). He practises verbal economy and understatement using the minimum number of words to create the maximum effect. He uses stylistic techniques like repetition, hidden metaphors, and objective and dramatic correlatives to produce the desired effects and to express more through fewer sentences. He plays with quotations which suggest and supplement meanings like T.S. Eliot, doing for prose what Eliot does for poetry. The Nobel Prize citation refers to his "style-making mastery" of the art of modern narration and praises him as "one of those who, honestly and undauntedly, reproduces the genuine features of the hard countenance of the age." His staccato style with its simple declarative sentences truthfully depicts the hard countenance of our times. This is on the surface only. Under the surface he presents unobtrusively to the discerning eye the philosophical theme of the futility of all human endeavour against the everlasting things, represented by the abiding earth and the Gulf-Stream or the perennial rivers or the flux of life itself which goes on undisturbed by the little insignificant human drama taking place on it like a little bubble appearing for a split second. He also focuses for the discerning eye the growth of the human soul.

A Farewell to Arms, like the other works of Hemingway, appeals at different levels. It is a story of war, a story of love, a story of the growth of the hero's soul, and a work of artistic excellence and stylistic achievement. It is a popular novel which is also a classic fit for enlightened appreciation.

Works Cited

PRIMARY WORKS

Ernest Hemingway. *In our Time.* New York: Charles Scribner's Sons, 1930 (First Pub. 1925).

——. *The Torrents of Spring.* New York: Charles Scribner's Sons, 1926.

——. *The Sun Also Rises.* New York: Charles Scribner's Sons, 1926.

——. *Men without Women.* New York: Charles Scribner's Sons, 1927.

——. *A Farewell to Arms.* Harmonds Worth: Penguin Books Ltd., 1968 (First Pub. 1929).

——. *Death in the Afternoon.* London: Jonathan Cape, 1963 (First Pub. 1932).

——. *Winner Take Nothing.* New York: Charles Scribner's Sons, 1933.

——. *Green Hills of Africa.* New York: Charles Scribner's Sons, 1935.

——. *To Have and Have Not.* New York: Charles Scribner's Sons, 1937.

——. *The Fifth Column and the First Forty-Nine Stories.* New York: Charles Scribner's Sons, 1938.

——. *For Whom the Bell Tolls.* New York: Charles Scribner's Sons, 1940.

——. *Men at War.* New York: Crown Publishers, 1942.

——. *Across the River and into the Trees.* New York: Charles Scribner's Sons, 1950.

——. *The Old Man and the Sea.* Harmondsworth: Penguin Books Ltd., 1966 (First Pub. 1952).

——. *A Moveable Feast*. New York: Charles Scribner's Sons, 1970. (First Pub. 1964).

——. *Islands in the Stream*. New York: Charles Scribner's Sons, 1970.

——. *The Garden of Eden*. New York: Charles Scribner's Sons, 1986.

——. *True at First Light*. New York: Charles Scribner's Sons, 1999.

——. Manuscripts of *A Farewell to Arms*. John F. Kennedy Presidential Library, Boston, Mass., 64/1—13 (Classification and Numbers by Jo August, the First Curator of the Hemingway Room).

SECONDARY WORKS

Anderson, Charles R. "Hemingway's Other Style", *Ernest Hemingway: Critiques of Four Major Novels*, ed. Carlos Baker. New York: Charles Scribner's Sons, 1962, 41-46.

Atkins, John. *The Art of Ernest Hemingway: His Work and Personality*. London: Spring Books, 1952.

Baker, Carlos. *Ernest Hemingway: The Writer as Artist*. Princeton: Princeton University Press, 1963 (3rd edition)

——, ed. *Ernest Hemingway: Selected Letters, 1917-1961*. New York: Charles Scribner's Sons, 1981.

Beach, Joseph Warren. "Ernest Hemingway: The Aesthetics of Simplicity", *American Fiction 1920-1940*. New York: Macmillan, 1941.

Beach, Sylvia. *Shakespeare and Company*. London: Faber and Faber, 1959.

Behlmer, Rudy, ed. *Memo from David O. Selznick*. New York: Viking, 1972.

Beja, Morris. *Film and Literature*. New York: Longman, 1970.

Benedictine Monks of St. Augustine's Abbey, Comp. *The Book of Saints: A Dictionary of Servants of God Canonized by the Catholic Church*. London: Adams and Charles Black, 197 (1921 edition).

Beversluis, John. "Dispelling the Romantic Myth: A Study of *A Farewell to Arms*." *The Hemingway Review*. Special *FTA* Issue, Vol. IX, No.1 (Fall 1989), 18-25.

Bishop, John Peale. "Homage to Hemingway", *After the Genteel Tradition: American Writers 1910-1930,* ed. Malcolm Cowley. Carbondale: Southern Illinois University Press, 1964.

Boyum, Joy Gould. *Double Exposure: Fiction into Film.* Calcutta: Sea Gull, 1985.

Brooks, Cleanth. "Man on his Moral Uppers", *The Hidden God: Studies in Hemingway, Faulkner, Yeats, Eliot and Warren.* New Haven: Yale University Press, 1963.

Burgum, Edwin Berry. "Ernest Hemingway and the Psychology of the Lost Generation", *Ernest Hemingway: The Man and his Work,* ed. J.K.M. McCaffery. New York: The World Publishing Company, 1950.

Campbell, Joseph. *The Hero with a Thousand Faces.* Princeton: Princeton University Press, 1968 (First Pub. 1949).

Carpenter, F.I. "Hemingway Achieves the Fifth Dimension", *Hemingway and His Critics: An International Anthology,* ed. Carlos Baker. New York: Hill and Wang, 1966.

Cooperman, Stanley. "Death and Cojones: Frederic Henry", *World War I and the American Novel.* Baltimore: John Hopkins University Press, 1967.

Cowley, Malcolm. "Nightmare and Ritual in Hemingway", *Hemingway: A Collection of Critical Essays,* ed. Robert P. Weeks, Englewood Cliffs (N.J.): Prentice Hall, 1962.

Dittmar, Linda. "Exultation or Excess? Hemingway the Author and Hemingway on Screen", *Ernest Hemingway: Centennial Essays,* ed. E. Nageswara Rao. Delhi: Pencraft International, 2000.

Eastman, Max. "Bull in the Afternoon", *Ernest Hemingway: The Man and His Work,* ed. J.K.M. McCaffery. New York: The World Publishing Company, 1950.

Edel, Leon. "The Art of Evasion", *Hemingway: A Collection of Critical Essays,* ed. Robert P. Weeks. Englewood Cliffs (N.J.): Prentice Hall, 1962.

Eliot, T.S. *The Sacred Wood: Essays on Poetry and Criticism.* London: Methuen & Co., 1950 (First Pub. 1920).

Fenton, Charles. *The Apprenticeship of Ernest Hemingway: The Early Years*. New York: The New American Library, 1961 (First Pub. 1954).

Fetterley, Judith. *The Resisting Reader: A Feminist Approach to American Fiction*. Bloomington: Indiana University Press, 1978.

Ganzel, Dewey. "*Cabestro* and *Vaquilla*: The Symbolic Structure of *The Sun Also Rises*." *Sewanee Review*, LXXVI (Winter 1968), 26-48.

Halliday, E.M. "Hemingway's Ambiguity: Symbolism and Irony", *Interpretations of American Literature,* ed. Charles Feidelson, Jr., and Paul Brodtkorb, Jr. New York: Oxford University Press, 1959, 207-319.

Hanrahan, Gene Z. *The Wild Years: Ernest Hemingway*. New York: Dell Publishing Co., 1962.

Hemingway, Leicester. *My Brother: Ernest Hemingway*. London: Weidenfield and Nicolson, 1962.

Hotchner, A.E. *Papa Hemingway*. New York: Random House, 1966.

Killinger, John. *Hemingway and the Dead Gods: A Study in Existentialism*. Kentucky: University of Kentucky Press, 1960.

Levin, Harry. "Observations on the Style of Ernest Hemingway." *Kenyon Review*, XIII (Autumn 1951).

Lewis Jr., Robert W. *Hemingway on Love*. Austin: University of Texas Press, 1965.

Lewis, Wyndham. "The Dumb Ox: A Study of Ernest Hemingway", *Men without Art*. London: Cassel, 1934.

Lodge, David. *Language of Fiction: Essays in Criticism and Verbal Analysis of the English Novel*. London: Routledge and Kegan Paul, 1966.

Lynn, Kenneth S. *Hemingway*. New York: Simon and Schuster, 1987.

Macleish, Archibald. *Time*, LXIV (December 13, 1954).

Maurois, Andre. "Ernest Hemingway", *Hemingway and His Critics: An International Anthology*, ed. Carlos Baker. New York: Hill and Wang, 1966.

Meloney, Michael F. "Ernest Hemingway: The Missing Third Dimension", *Hemingway and His Critics: An International Anthology,* ed. Carlos Baker. New York: Hill and Wang, 1966.

Morris, Wright. *The Territory Ahead.* New York: Atheneum, 1963.

Naik, M.K. "Thematic Structure in *A Farewell to Arms*", *The Indian Journal of English Studies, VIII* (March 1968), 79-82.

O'Faolain, San. "A Clean Well-Lighted Place", *Hemingway: A Collection of Critical Essays,* ed. Robert P. Weeks. Englewood Cliffs (N.J.): Prentice Hall, 1962.

Oldsey, Bernard. *Hemingway's Hidden Craft: The Writing of A Farewell to Arms.* University Park: Penn. State University Press, 1979.

Oliver, Charles M., ed. *A Moving Picture Feast: A Filmgoer's Hemingway.* London & New York: Praeger, 1989.

Phillips, Gene D. *Hemingway and Film.* New York: Frederick Ungar, 1980.

Plimpton, George. "An Interview with Ernest Hemingway", *Hemingway and His Critics: An International Anthology,* ed. Carlos Baker. New York: Hill and Wang, 1966.

Rama Rao, P.G. *Ernest Hemingway: A Study in Narrative Technique.* New Delhi: S. Chand and Company, 1980.

Reynolds, Michael S. *Hemingway's First War: The Making of A Farewell to Arms.* Princeton: Princeton University Press, 1976.

Ross, Lillian. "How Do You Like It Now, Gentlemen?", *Hemingway: A Collection of Critical Essays,* ed. Robert P. Weeks. Englewood Cliffs (N.J.): Prentice Hall, 1962.

Rouch, John S. "Jake Barnes as Narrator", *Modern Fiction Studies,* II (Winter 1965-66), 361-70.

Rovit, Earl. *Ernest Hemingway.* New Haven: College and University Press, 1963.

Sanderson, Stewart. *Ernest Hemingway.* Edinburgh: Oliver and Boyd Ltd., 1961.

Schorer, Mark. "With Grace under Pressure", *Ernest Hemingway: Critiques of Four Major Novels*, ed., Carlos Baker. New York: Charles Scribner's Sons, 1962.

Spilka, Mark. "The Death of Love in *The Sun Also Rises*." *Hemingway and his Critics: An International Anthology*, ed. Carlos Baker. New York: Hill and Wang, 1966.

Stallman, R.W. *The Houses That James Built and Other Literary Studies*. Michigan State University Press, 1964.

Stein, Gertrude. *The Autobiography of Alice B. Toklas*. New York: Vintage Books, Alfred A. Knopf and Random House, 1961 (First Pub. 1933).

Stoneback, H.R. "'Lovers' Sonnets Turn'd to Holy Psalms': The Soul's Song of Providence, the Scandal of Suffering, and Love in *A Farewell to Arms*." *The Hemingway Review* (Special *FTA* Issue). Vol. IX, No. 1 (Fall 1989), 33-76.

Waldmeir, Joseph. "*Confiteor Hominem*: Ernest Hemingway's Religion of Man," *Hemingway: A Collection of Critical Essays,* ed. Robert P. Weeks. Englewood Cliffs (N.J): Prentice Hall, 1962.

Warren, Robert Penn. "Introduction," *A Farewell to Arms*. New York: Charles Scribner's Sons, 1957.

Welland, D.S.R. "Hemingway's English Reputation", *The Literary Reputation of Hemingway in Europe*, ed. Roger Asselineau. New York: New York University Press, 1965.

White, William, ed. *By-Line: Ernest Hemingway*. New York: Bantam Books Inc., 1968.

Wilson, Edmund *Axel's Castle: A Study in the Imaginative Literature of 1870-1930*. New York: Charles Scribner's Sons, 1950.

——. "Hemingway: Gauge of Morale", *The Wound and the Bow: Seven Studies in Literature*. New York: Oxford University Press, 1965, 174-97.

Young, Phillip. *Ernest Hemingway: A Reconsideration*. University Park, Pa: Pennsylvania State University Press, 1966.

Index